LIFE SKILLS FOR TWEENS

WORKBOOK

How to Cook, Make Friends, Be Self Confident and Healthy

Everything a Pre Teen Should Know to Be a Brilliant Teenager

FERNE BOWE

TABLE OF CONTENTS

INTRODUCTION

Congratulations... you're a tween! And in no time at all, you'll be a teen!

These are exciting times, but it is also a time of transition. You're moving from childhood to adulthood, and that can be a bit scary. With so many new challenges coming your way, it's perfectly normal to feel a bit overwhelmed.

That's why we created this workbook — to help you learn the life skills you need to succeed as a tween and beyond. It's packed with activities, worksheets, illustrations, and tips to help you become more confident and capable in all aspects of your life.

From managing money and cooking meals to staying positive and developing friendships — this workbook is here to guide you every step of the way.

But before we begin... What are life skills, and why do you need them?

Life skills are the abilities and knowledge that help us effectively navigate and handle the challenges and responsibilities of everyday life. They help us communicate effectively, solve problems, make decisions, and manage our time and resources. They include everything from practical skills like cooking a meal to more emotional skills such as staying positive or understanding emotions.

Life skills are essential for several reasons. They help us become more independent and confident, which can lead to greater success both in our personal life and career. They also ensure that we make better decisions when faced with difficult situations.

Imagine that you are building a house. Strong life skills are like having a solid foundation of bricks that will support you as you grow and mature. This foundation will help you navigate the challenges and responsibilities of everyday life with confidence and ease.

On the other hand, if you don't have strong life skills, it's like having a weak foundation of bricks. Your house (or, in this case, your life) may still stand, but it will be more prone to challenges and setbacks, and you may feel less equipped to handle them.

So think of developing strong life skills as a solid foundation for your future. The more bricks (or life skills) you have in your foundation, the more prepared and confident you will be to take on whatever comes your way.

That's what this book is here to help you do: build that foundation of life skills. So let's get started!

You have an exciting journey ahead of you!

HOW TO USE THIS BOOK

This book is a workbook that accompanies Life Skills for Tweens. While the other book provides a more detailed overview of the various life skills, this workbook offers activities and worksheets to help put those skills into practice.

The chapters in this book are divided into different categories, such as Personal Development, Friends & Relationships, Emotions, School & Learning, etc. Each chapter then has several activities and worksheets that you can use to help cultivate the life skills that are relevant to that particular category.

We recommend starting with the first chapter and working your way through each of them in order. This will ensure that you cover all the primary life skills necessary for success as a tween and beyond. But feel free to skip around or focus on specific topics as needed.

Let's get started! We know you'll love learning these life skills, and we can't wait to see what amazing things you accomplish with them. Good luck, and have fun! :)

You got this. Let's go!

CHAPTER 1

PERSONAL DEVELOPMENT

Are you ready to conquer the world?

Chances are you're already well on your way, but having a solid foundation of personal development skills will help you get there faster.

This chapter will explore essential life skills needed for personal growth and success.

We'll start by exploring ways to manage your time effectively, set goals and stay motivated.

Then we'll dive into building self-confidence and self-esteem.

By the end of this chapter, you'll have all the tools you need to start your journey toward becoming the best 'you' possible!

Let's get started on this exciting journey — you're in control of your future, and everything is possible if you put your mind to it.

HOW TO BE A TIME MANAGEMENT SUPERSTAR

Time is one of your most valuable resources. There are only 24 hours in a day. You might be asleep for 10 of those, leaving 14 hours to juggle school, homework, extra-curricular activities, and chores. How do you fit it all in?

Let's start with the basics.

How do you spend your time?

Since time is limited, it's important to know how you spend your time. Are you spending too much time on social media or playing video games? Or maybe you're having trouble managing your school work and extracurricular activities.

Keeping a time log is useful to help you understand how you spend your time. Write down everything you do and how long it takes for one week. Mark next to each item if it is a high-priority or low-priority activity.

- **High-priority activities** are things you must complete for school, family needs, or other essential commitments.

- **Low-priority activities** include watching TV, playing video games, etc.

Once you have completed your time log, it's time to assess how much of your time is spent on high-priority activities and how much is spent on low-priority activities. This will give you an idea of where to make adjustments to better manage your time.

For instance, if you're spending too much time on your phone (a low-priority activity), a good goal might be to limit yourself to 30 minutes a day.

HOW TO BE A

TIME MANAGEMENT SUPERSTAR

ACTIVITY 1 - HOW DO YOU USE YOUR TIME?

Write down all the activities you do in a typical day and how long they take. Include everything, even the time playing games. Mark if it is a high-priority or low-priority activity.

Daily Activities Record				
DATE: _____				
Start Time	End Time	Total Time Spent	Activity	Priority H/L

Continue here...

Start Time	End Time	Total Time Spent	Activity	Priority H/L

Now take a marker and highlight all the low priority tasks that you did today.

TIME MANAGEMENT SUPERSTAR

ACTIVITY 2 - TIME IMPROVEMENT

How can you improve your time management? Write down 5 low-priority activities from your log & how you could reduce time on them. For instance, if you're spending too much time online, a good goal might be to limit yourself to 30 mins. a day.

You're a STAR

HOW TO PRIORITIZE TASKS

It's easy to get overwhelmed with everything you need to do. Knowing what needs to be done first and what can wait until later is vital to managing your time effectively.

Start by creating a list of all the tasks that you need to complete. Then prioritize them into three categories: Urgent, Important, and Can Wait.

Urgent tasks must be done immediately, such as finishing a school assignment before the deadline or helping with a pressing family chore.

Important tasks may not necessarily have a specific time limit but must be done. These could include studying for an upcoming test or spending time with family.

Can Wait tasks can be done later, such as playing a game or watching TV.

HOW TO BE A

TIME MANAGEMENT SUPERSTAR

ACTIVITY 3 - PRIORITIZING TASKS

Make a list of all the tasks you need to do. Use this worksheet to prioritize them by importance or urgency.

URGENT!

Things that need immediate attention.

IMPORTANT!

Things that that are important but don't need to be done right away.

CAN WAIT!

Things that aren't urgent or important and can wait a few more days.

Now that you understand the basics of time management and prioritization, it's time to set some goals! Setting goals can keep you motivated and on track toward achieving your dreams.

HOW TO SET GOALS

Goal setting is deciding what you want to accomplish and planning how to achieve it. It's like setting a destination for a trip — you need to know where you want to go and then figure out the best route to get there.

Setting goals helps you stay focused, motivated, and on track to achieve your desired results. Goals also give you something to work towards. When you encounter challenges along the way, you can use those challenges as learning experiences to reach your ultimate goal.

When you set goals, it's essential to make them specific and achievable.

For example, instead of saying, "I want to get better at soccer," you might set a specific goal like "I want to improve my dribbling skills so I can score more goals in my soccer games."

This way, you have a clear target to work towards, and you'll be able to measure your progress.

It's also a good idea to set both short-term and long-term goals.

- **Short-term goals** are things you want to accomplish in the near future, like improving your soccer skills by the end of the season.

- **Long-term goals** are things you want to achieve in the future, like becoming the best soccer player in your league.

SET GOALS!

WHAT IS GOAL SETTING?

Goal setting is the process of deciding what you want to accomplish, and making a plan for how to achieve it.

WHY IS IT IMPORTANT?

Setting goals helps you stay focused, motivated, and on track to achieve your desired results.

GOAL SETTING IN 4 SIMPLE STEPS:

1. WRITE DOWN YOUR BIG GOAL.

2. MAKE YOUR GOAL S.M.A.R.T.

3. CREATE A PLAN OF ACTION.
-Identify possible challenges & how you'll overcome them
-Be inspired & stay motivated

4. DO IT!

HOW TO SET S.M.A.R.T. GOALS

When setting a goal, it's important to ensure it is realistic and achievable. Start by creating a "SMART" goal — Specific, Measurable, Attainable, Relevant, and Time-bound.

For example,

I want to finish my math homework by 9 pm each night this week.

This goal is **specific** in that you know exactly what you need to do, it's **measurable** (you can check if the goal has been achieved), **attainable** (finishing math homework in one night is very doable), **relevant** (it's related to your studies and important to your success in school), and **time-bound** (you have a deadline of 9pm each night).

You might need help with defining specific goals to begin with. To help you, try answering the five W's: Who, when, where, what, and which. For example:

Who: I
When: this week
Where: at home
What: finish my math homework
Which: by 9 pm each night.

By answering these five questions, you will have a clearer idea of what you want to achieve and how you plan on achieving it.

Creating SMART goals will help you stay on track, use your time more effectively, and achieve the desired results.

Have a go at creating your own SMART goals, and see what you can achieve!

SET GOALS!
DREAMS & GOAL SETTING

WHAT ARE YOUR LONG-TERM DREAMS?
Imagine what you could achieve in 10-20 years. Write down some of your dreams.

1
2
3
4

5
6
7
8

SHORT-TERM GOALS
Based on your dreams, what are some shorter term goals you would like to achieve.

1
2
3

4
5
6

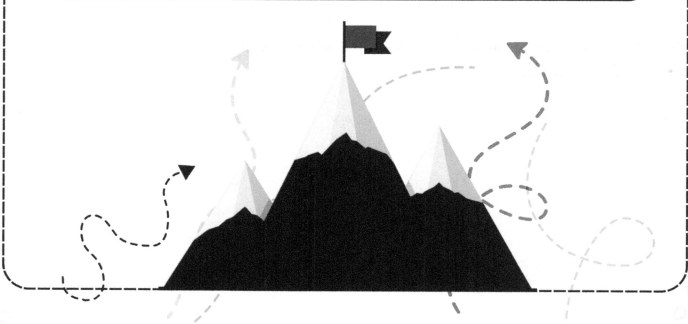

SET GOALS!

HOW **SMART** IS YOUR GOAL?

S specific

A specific goal tells you exactly what you want to accomplish. For example, instead of, "I want to get better at soccer," a specific goal might be, "I want to improve my dribbling skills so I can score more goals."

M measurable

A measurable goal has criteria for tracking your progress. For example, you might want to track how many goals you score in your soccer games to see if you're getting better.

A attainable

An attainable goal is something that you can actually accomplish. It might be a bit challenging, but it's not impossible.

R relevant

A relevant goal is important to you and aligns with your interests. For example, if you really enjoy and care about soccer, then setting a goal to improve your soccer skills would be relevant.

T time-bound

A time-bound goal has a specific deadline or timeline. This helps you stay focused and motivated to achieve your goal. For example, you might set a goal to improve your soccer skills by the end of the season.

SET GOALS!
CREATE YOUR OWN SMART GOAL

It's time to make your goals S.M.A.R.T. Answer the questions below.

S *specific*
What exactly do you want to accomplish? Tip: try to answer the five 'W's.' Who, when, where, what, which.

 **M** *measurable*
How will you know when you have reached your goal? Tip: try to answer 'How much' or 'How many' questions.

 **A** *attainable*
Is achieving this goal realistic? Do you have the ability, skills, and resources? If not, how will you get them?

R *relevant*
Why is this goal important? Tip: try to describe why it matters to you.

T *time-bound*
When will you achieve the goal? Tip: try to answer the question 'When?'

READY, SET, ACTION!

Now you have your SMART goal try breaking it down into mini-goals or milestones. These are smaller steps that, when combined, will lead to you achieving your ultimate goal.

MINI GOALS OR MILESTONES	HOW LONG WILL THIS TAKE?	TARGET DEADLINE

OVERCOME OBSTACLES LIKE A PRO!

Staying on track can be difficult when trying to achieve a goal. What are the possible obstacles you might face? How will you be able to overcome these challenges if they arise?

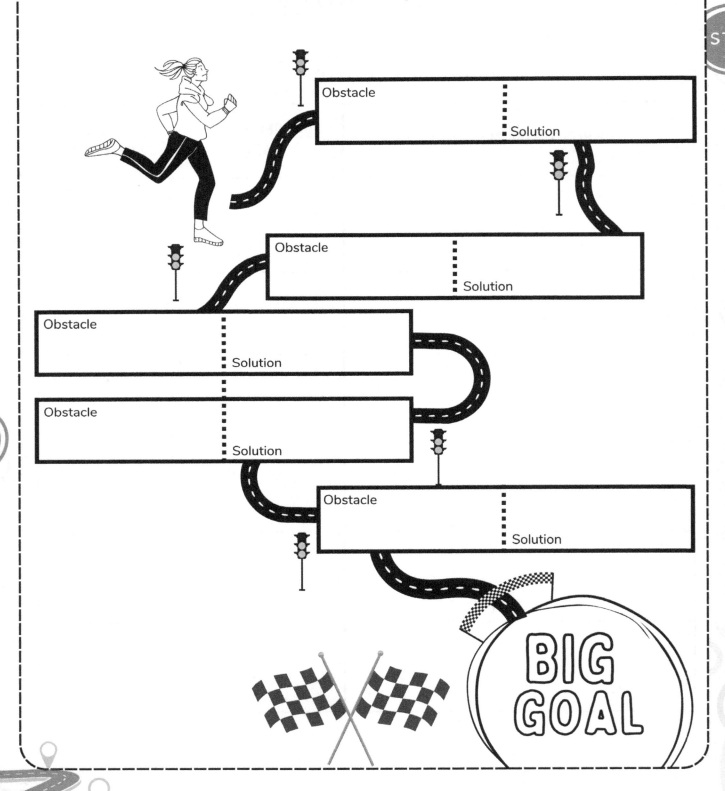

Obstacle ⋮ Solution

Obstacle ⋮ Solution

Obstacle ⋮ Solution

Obstacle ⋮ Solution

Obstacle ⋮ Solution

BIG GOAL

STOP

STAY MOTIVATED!

Create a collage of motivation. Any time you feel like giving up, refer back to your collage for extra motivation.

HOW TO...

Paste a photo or draw a picture of a role model - someone you look up to

What is your favorite MOTIVATIONAL song?

What book inspires you?

Insert your very own Motivational Quote

HOW TO BUILD CONFIDENCE

Setting goals and achieving them is a great feeling. When you set a goal and work towards it, you're taking control and showing yourself that you can achieve what you set your mind to. This can be a great source of pride and accomplishment and can help boost your confidence and self-esteem.

Of course, there will be times when you fail to reach your goals. But that doesn't mean you should give up and stop trying. Instead, look at what went wrong and use it as a learning experience to become better equipped to reach those goals next time.

Stepping outside your comfort zone

One way to build confidence is to push yourself outside your comfort zone.

Your comfort zone is the area of your life in which you feel safe, secure, and comfortable. It's the place where it feels like nothing can go wrong, and you don't have to take any risks.

For example, if you're good at soccer and enjoy playing with your friends, the soccer field might be part of your comfort zone. Or if you love reading and spending time with your family, your bedroom or living room might be part of your comfort zone.

Your comfort zone can be a great place to relax and recharge, but it can also hold you back if you never step outside of it.

Sometimes, it's important to challenge yourself and try new things, even if it means stepping out of your comfort zone. It could be anything from taking a cooking class or joining a club to signing up for an after-school program or volunteering in the community. This can help you build confidence and expose you to different experiences that can lead to personal growth and development.

For example, if you don't typically get involved in school activities, try joining a club or team and see how it feels! Chances are, the more you push yourself, the more you'll develop a sense of confidence and accomplishment.

Using the worksheet, make a list of activities that are just outside your comfort zone and make a plan to give them a try. Here are a few ideas to help you get started:

- **Try a new hobby**: Trying a new hobby or activity can be a great way to challenge yourself and step out of your comfort zone. This might be something you've always been interested in or something new.

- **Join a new club or team**: Joining a new club or team can be a great way to meet new people and try something new. It might be a little intimidating initially, but it can also be a lot of fun and a great way to challenge yourself.

- **Speak up in class**: If you're usually quiet in class, try speaking up more often. This can be a great way to challenge yourself and boost your confidence.

- **Volunteer**: Volunteering for a cause you care about can be a great way to make a difference and step out of your comfort zone. It might involve interacting with new people or trying new things, but it can also be a very rewarding experience.

- **Take a trip**: Traveling to a new place, especially somewhere you've never been before, can be a great way to step out of your comfort zone. It might be a little intimidating at first, but it can also be a lot of fun and a great way to experience new things.

Remember, no matter what happens, take pride in the fact that you stepped out of your comfort zone and gave it a go. It's all part of the process of learning and growing. And in the end, that's what life skills are all about — gaining knowledge and developing the ability to take on anything that comes your way!

COMFORT ZONE
CHALLENGE

In the bottom circle, list everything in your comfort zone. Now try to think of new things you could do to push yourself outside your comfort zone. Add these into the growth zone.

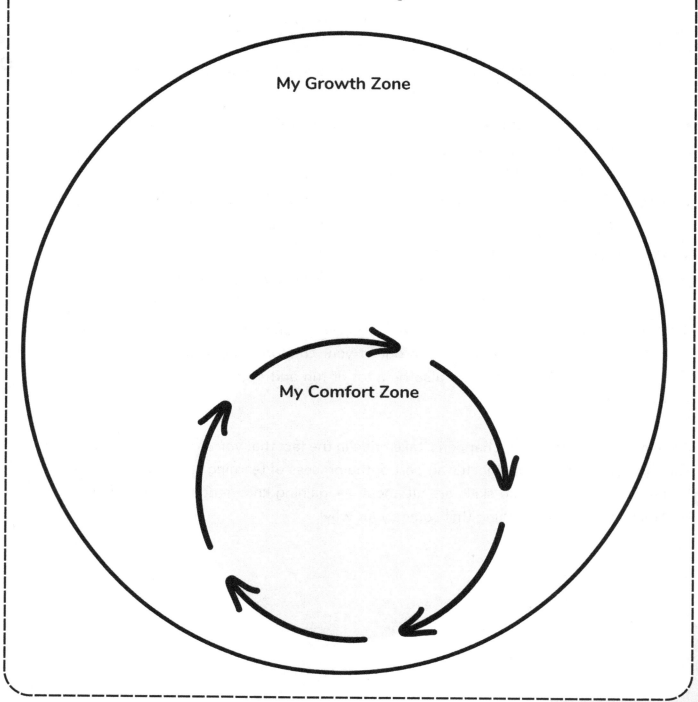

My Growth Zone

My Comfort Zone

CHAPTER 2

FRIENDS & RELATIONSHIPS

Good friends are essential to a healthy, happy life. They provide support, encouragement, and a sense of belonging.

Having strong friendships is important at any age, but it can be especially important as you navigate the tween and teen years. During this time, you may be experiencing new challenges and changes, and having friends who understand and support you can make all the difference.

TYPES OF FRIENDSHIPS

Of course, not all friends are the same.

Recognizing the different types of relationships and connections can help you build positive relationships that will last into adulthood!

- **Best Friends**: These are the closest friends in your life and the ones you can always count on. You trust them. You share a deep bond and support each other through thick and thin.

- **Friends**: These are people you are friendly with but perhaps don't share the same level of trust and intimacy as you do with your best friends.

- **Acquaintances**: These are people you know but don't have a close relationship with. They might be people you run into at school or in the community.

- **Online Friends**: This type of friendship is growing as more people use the internet and social media. While making real connections online is possible, remember that not all online friends are who they say they are, so use caution.

- **'So-called Friends'**: These are people you may think of as friends but don't really have your best interests at heart. They might be manipulative or take advantage of you. You might also refer to them as 'bad friends.'

TYPES OF FRIENDSHIPS

BEST FRIENDS

These are the closest friends in your life and the ones you can always count on. You trust them. You share a deep bond and support each other through thick and thin.

FRIENDS

These are people you are friendly with but perhaps don't share the same level of trust and intimacy as you do with your best friends.

ACQUAINTANCES

These are people you know but don't have a close relationship with. They might be people you run into at school or in the community

ONLINE FRIENDS

This type of friendship is growing as more people use social media. While making real connections online is possible, remember that not all online friends are whom they say they are, so use caution.

'SO-CALLED' FRIENDS

You may consider these people friends, but they don't always have your best interests at heart. They might be manipulative or take advantage of you.

Good friends vs. bad friends

As you have seen above, not all friends are created equal. We all have different personalities and values, so it's helpful to understand the difference between good and bad friends.

- **Good friends** are respectful, supportive, loyal, kind, and honest. They should be someone you can trust with your deepest thoughts and feelings. Good friends will make you feel better when you're down, celebrate your successes, and lift you up when you need it.

- **Bad friends** might be manipulative or take advantage of you. They may be rude and unsupportive and spread rumors or gossip about others. These types of friendships can harm your mental health and self-esteem.

It's helpful to take some time to evaluate who your true friends are and if they make you feel good or bad. You don't need negative people in your life, so don't be afraid to move on from the wrong friendships and find new ones that bring out the best in you.

GOOD FRIENDS VS. BAD FRIENDS

What makes a good friend or a bad friend? Write them in the boxes below.

People I want to hang out
with should...

People I don't want to
hang out with might...

HOW TO MEET PEOPLE AND MAKE NEW FRIENDS

As you get older, you will face new situations, and your friendships will evolve or change. Learning to break the ice, meet new people, and maintain and build meaningful relationships are essential life skills that can help you now and in the future.

Breaking the ice

Often, the most challenging part of making a new friend is getting started. Breaking the ice and introducing yourself to someone can be intimidating, but it doesn't have to be! Have a look at the sheet below. It's filled with different icebreaker conversation starters to help you get the ball rolling.

In addition to the icebreakers, here are some tips to help make meeting new people easier:

- **Smile** and look friendly

- **Make eye contact** when talking

- **Introduce yourself** with an interesting or funny fact about yourself

- **Ask questions** about the person you're talking to

- **Be yourself** and be confident!

Of course, only some people you meet will become good friends. Don't be discouraged; just keep being yourself and meet new people. You don't need large groups of friends to be happy, and it's important to remember that quality matters over quantity.

BREAKING THE ICE
CONVERSATION STARTERS

BELOW ARE SOME CONVERSATION STARTERS TO HELP YOU BREAK THE ICE WHEN YOU MEET NEW PEOPLE. THEY ARE ALL OPEN-ENDED QUESTIONS THAT ALLOW THE OTHER PERSON TO SHARE A BIT ABOUT THEMSELVES.

"What's your favorite hobby?"	"Do you have any brothers or sisters?"	"What's your favorite thing to do with your friends?"
"Do you have any pets?"	"What's your favorite subject in school?"	"Do you have any upcoming plans or events you're excited about?"
"What's your favorite book / movie / tv show?"	"What do you like to do in your free time?"	"Who's your favorite youtuber?"
"Do you play any sports or instruments?"	"What do you like most about your school/town/community?"	"If you could travel anywhere in the world, where would you go?"

REMEMBER, THE KEY TO BREAKING THE ICE IS TO BE FRIENDLY AND APPROACHABLE, AND TO SHOW GENUINE INTEREST IN THE OTHER PERSON.

Finding the right friends

When looking for a friend, it can help to have an idea of some of the qualities you're looking for

- Are they kind and trustworthy?

- Do they share your interests and values?

- Do they make you feel good about yourself?

- Will they be a positive influence in your life?

Look for friends with similar views and values as yours, who share your interests and hobbies, and who you can trust and rely on.

WANTED:

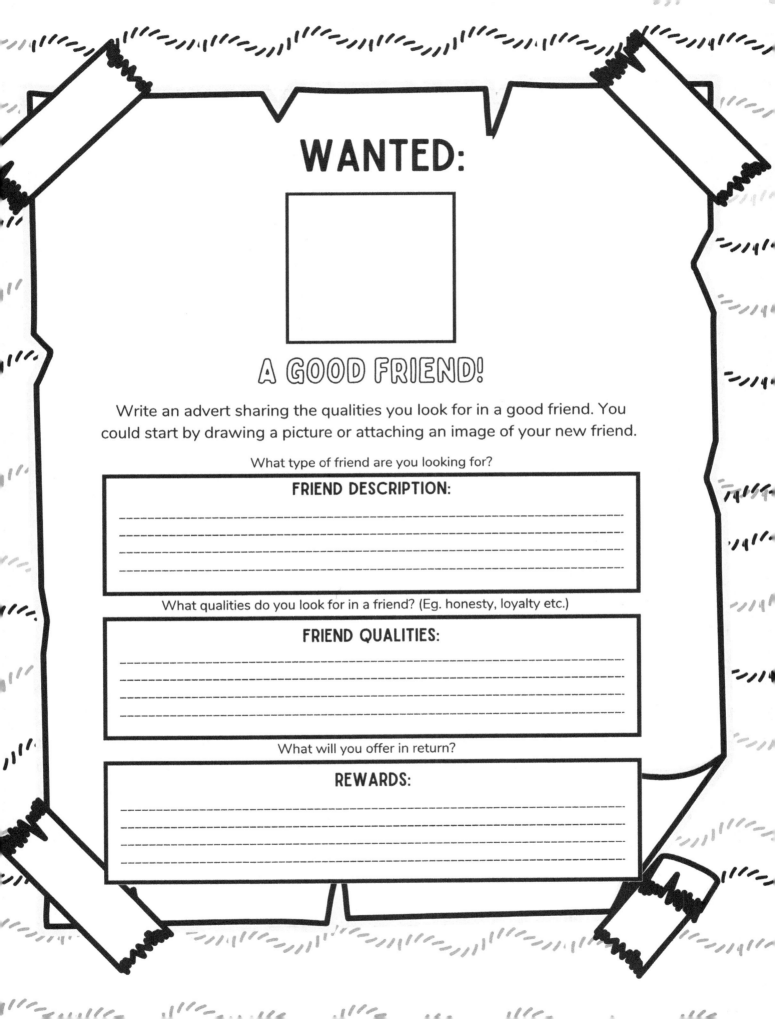

A GOOD FRIEND!

Write an advert sharing the qualities you look for in a good friend. You could start by drawing a picture or attaching an image of your new friend.

What type of friend are you looking for?

FRIEND DESCRIPTION:

_____
_____
_____
_____

What qualities do you look for in a friend? (Eg. honesty, loyalty etc.)

FRIEND QUALITIES:

_____
_____
_____
_____

What will you offer in return?

REWARDS:

_____
_____
_____
_____

MAINTAINING FRIENDSHIPS

Once you have found the right friends, it's important to maintain the relationship by staying in touch, supporting each other, respecting boundaries, and having fun together!

Good communication is vital in any friendship, so be honest and open. If you have a problem or conflict with a friend, try to talk about it instead of avoiding it or letting it fester.

Remember that although friends can come and go, true friendships last forever! If both of you are willing to try to maintain the relationship, it will be worth it in the end.

Managing conflict

Having disagreements is a normal part of any friendship. Even the closest friends can sometimes have arguments or misunderstand each other. When this happens, it's important to remember to stay calm and be respectful while trying to solve the problem.

If you are having a disagreement with your friend, here are some tips to help manage the conflict:

- **Communicate clearly** and calmly.
- **Listen to each other** without judging or interrupting.
- **Respect each other's opinions.**
- **Focus on the issue** and don't bring up past grievances.
- **Be willing to compromise** or find a solution for both of you.

Of course, not all conflicts can be resolved, but it's important to remember that not everyone will agree all the time. Having healthy conflict-resolution skills can help you build better relationships with your friends and others.

THE DIFFERENT APPROACHES

Having disagreements is a normal part of any friendship. When this happens, try to stay calm and be respectful while trying to solve the problem.

There are broadly 5 different approaches people take. Some are more positive than others. Have a look through them. Which do you think is right for you?

DIFFERENT APPROACHES:	WHAT IT MEANS:	EXAMPLE:
COMPETING	Trying to win the conflict by getting your own way no matter what.	Refusing to listen to each other's opinions.
ACCOMMODATING	Giving in to the other person and putting their needs above your own.	Apologizing even if you didn't do anything wrong.
AVOIDING	Is when someone decides not to address the issue and instead tries to ignore it.	Pretending like nothing ever happened.
COLLABORATING	Is a more positive way of managing conflict as it involves both parties working together to find a solution that works for everyone.	Brainstorming ideas and coming up with compromises that suit both people's needs.
COMPROMISING	Is when both parties agree to give up something in order to find a solution that works for both of them.	Agreeing to do one activity together, and then doing different activities separately.

MANAGING CONFLICT

SCENARIO:

You're on a school project with a friend and disagree on how much time each should spend working on it. Your friend thinks their contributions should be recognized, and you think they should be taking the project more seriously.

WHAT APPROACHES COULD YOU TAKE?	HOW MIGHT IT MAKE THEM FEEL?

CHAPTER 3

EMOTIONS

Happy, sad, angry — these are just a few of the many emotions you may be feeling as a tween.

It's normal to handle all kinds of emotions, but it can be confusing to try and understand them all. This chapter will discuss different feelings and how to manage them healthily.

Having emotional control is a valuable skill to have as you grow older. Understanding your emotions and how to express them in healthy ways can help you build better relationships with others, stay focused on tasks, and manage stress better. So let's jump right into it!

UNDERSTANDING YOUR EMOTIONS

Understanding your emotions and moods is the first step to managing them. When feeling a particular emotion, it can be helpful to name it and think about what caused it. This will help you identify patterns in your emotions and recognize possible solutions that could reduce stress or conflict.

Sometimes, it may seem like an emotion has come out of nowhere — but if you take the time to think about it, you'll find that there's usually a reason for your feelings. It could be something from the past, a current situation, or even something in the future.

EMOTIONS

DRAW THE EMOTIONS

Draw the emotions on the faces below

HAPPY	SUPRISED	ANGRY

SCARED	FEARFUL	CONFUSED

STRESSED	CONTENT	GRATEFUL

THE "MOOD" WALL

21-day mood monitoring. Fill out each brick in the color that represents your mood for that day.

Mood Color Scale: Give each mood a different color

Terrible   V. Bad   Bad   Okay   Good   Great   Awesome
◯   ◯   ◯   ◯   ◯   ◯   ◯

1	2	3
4	5	6
7	8	9
10	11	12	13
14	15	16
17	18	19
20	21

What made you feel good? What made you feel bad? Note them down below:

....

....

....

ANGER

It's normal to feel angry sometimes. But it's important to know how to manage it to maintain healthy relationships with those around you. Let's look at some ways to manage anger:

- **Take a break** — If you can, step away from the situation and take time for yourself. This will give you time to cool off and think about the situation more rationally.

- **Talk it out** — Talking to someone you trust can help express your anger without hurting others or yourself. It can also provide perspective on the situation, which might help reduce the intensity of your anger.

- **Practice mindfulness** — Taking a few moments to pay attention to your breathing can help calm you down and manage your anger.

Remember: Anger is natural, but it's essential to learn how to express it in healthy ways to keep your relationships with people strong and positive.

UNDERSTANDING ANGER

It's normal to feel angry sometimes. But it's important to know how to manage it in order to maintain healthy relationships with those around you.

Why are you angry?

How did you handle it?

What were the consequences of your anger?

How could you have handled it better?

What would have happened if you handled it this way?

ANGER MANAGEMENT
HOW TO HANDLE ANGER

Below are some possible ways to deal with anger. The next time you feel angry, why not try one of these techniques.

Draw your Anger

Do 20 Jumping Jacks

Take 20 Deep Breaths

Use Squeeze Balls

Talk to Someone

Count to 100

Listen to Music

Play Outside

Walk Away

ANGER --> CALM

THINGS THAT CALM YOUR ANGER

Did you use some of the techniques in the previous worksheet? Mark down below what works best for you to calm your anger.

STRESS & ANXIETY

It's normal to feel stressed or anxious sometimes. In fact, they are both common emotions that many people experience. While they are related, they are not the same thing.

Stress is a normal response to challenges and demands. It is the body's way of preparing to deal with a situation that requires extra effort or attention. Stress can be caused by various factors, such as school, family, friends, or changes in your life.

On the other hand, anxiety is a feeling of worry, nervousness, or unease about something that may happen. Anxiety is often accompanied by physical symptoms such as increased heart rate, difficulty breathing, and stomach discomfort. Anxiety can be caused by stress or other factors and can range from mild to severe.

It's important to remember that some stress and anxiety are normal and can even be helpful in certain situations. *For example, a little bit of stress can help you stay focused and motivated, and a small amount of anxiety can help you stay alert and prepared.* However, excessive stress or anxiety can harm your physical and mental health.

To manage stress and anxiety, taking care of yourself and finding healthy ways to cope with challenges and demands is important. This might include:

- **Exercise**: Physical activity is a great way to relieve stress and improve your mood. Going for a walk or run, playing sports, or dancing to your favorite music are all fun ways to get moving.

- **Relaxation techniques**: Relaxation techniques such as deep breathing, yoga, or meditation can help calm your mind and release tension.

- **Talk to someone**: Sometimes, it can be helpful to talk to a friend or family member about what's stressing you out. They can offer a different perspective and provide support.

- **Write it down**: Writing down your thoughts and feelings can help you to clear your mind and make sense of what's troubling you.

- **Laugh and smile**: Laughter is a powerful stress-buster. Watch a funny movie, read a humorous book or spend time with friends who make you laugh.

- **Get enough sleep**: A good night's sleep can help you feel refreshed and better able to cope with stress.

- **Set realistic goals**: Break big tasks into smaller, more manageable chunks. Setting small achievable goals helps reduce stress.

- **Be creative**: Whether drawing, painting, writing, or composing music, expressing yourself creatively can be a great way to cope with stress.

For example, suppose you have a big test coming up instead of stressing about it for days. In that case, you can break it down and make a study schedule, take short breaks to relax, and do something you enjoy, like listening to music. Or, if you are feeling overwhelmed, you can take a few deep breaths and close your eyes for a few minutes of quiet time.

Using these techniques, you'll be better equipped to manage stress and maintain your emotional well-being. Remember, it's essential to find what works for you and not be afraid to seek help.

ANXIETY & MY BODY

How do you feel when you're anxious or stressed? Color in the reactions, or add your own in the blank circles below.

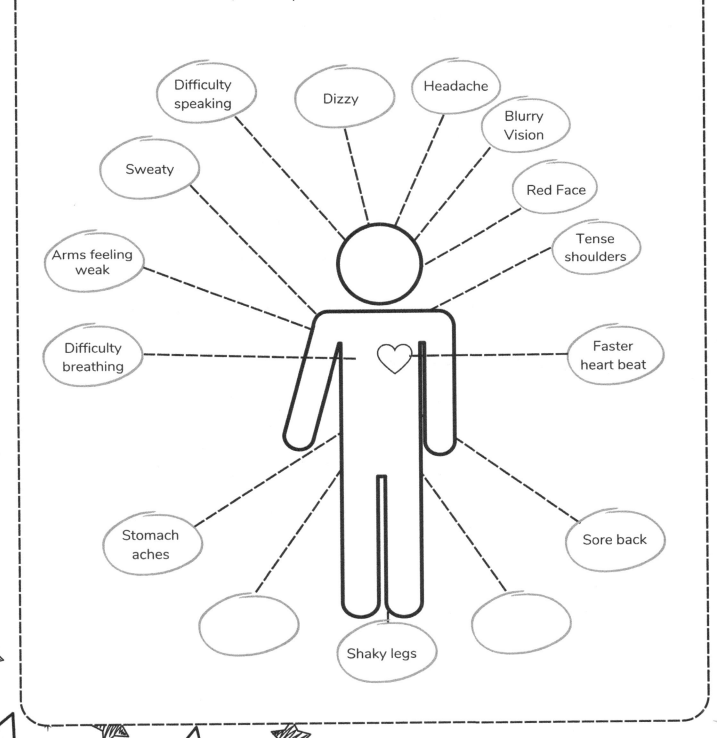

STRESS & ANXIETY

INSTEAD OF...

How can you react differently to stress? When you are next feeling anxious or stressed, use this worksheet to come up with some different coping skills.

WHEN I NEXT FEEL ANXIOUS, INSTEAD OF...

(Write down how you usually cope with stress)

....

....

....

....

....

I WILL USE THESE COPING SKILLS...

(Mark off the different coping skills you use)

☐ ....

☐ ....

☐ ....

☐ ....

☐ ....

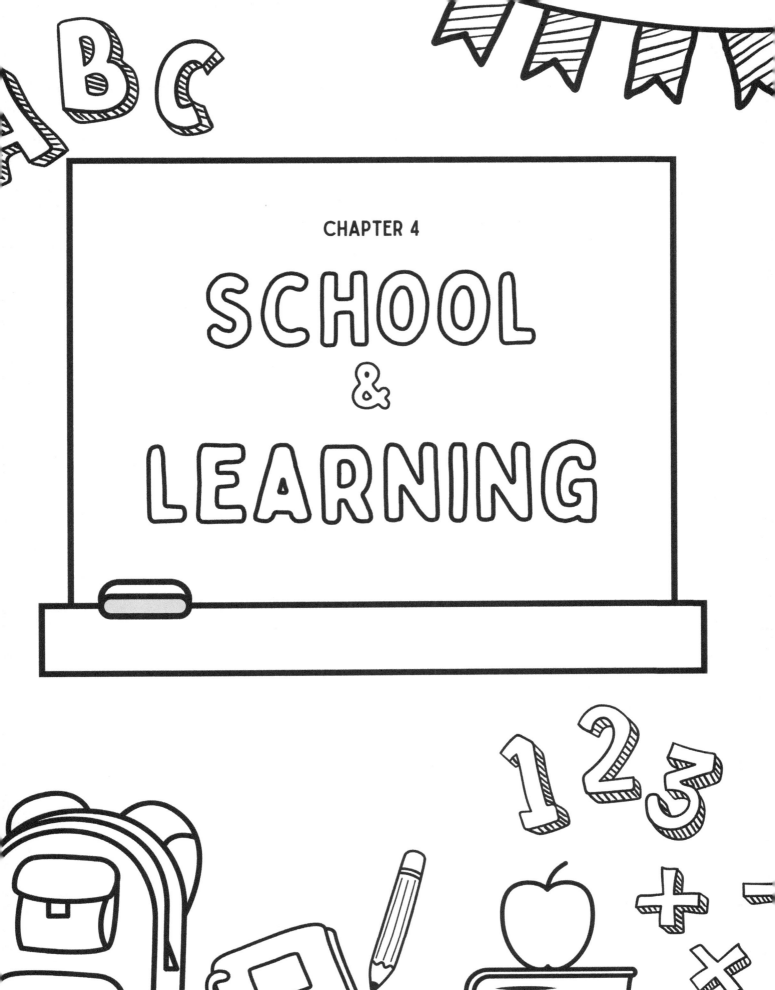

CHAPTER 4

SCHOOL & LEARNING

School is an integral part of your life and can be a rewarding and challenging experience.

It is where you learn new things, discover your interests and passions, and develop skills. It's also where you make friends and become part of a community.

Of course, school can be challenging at times. It can be difficult to stay motivated during classes or when dealing with other difficulties. But school is a big step in the lifelong learning process. It's a valuable investment in your future. The skills and knowledge you gain in school will serve you well in your future studies and career and can help you achieve your goals and dreams.

And it's about so much more than just getting good grades. **School is about developing skills, gaining knowledge, and growing as a person.**

This chapter will look at tips and strategies to help you succeed in school.

MEET THE STUDENT

Complete the worksheet below, listing your top skills and the achievements you are most proud of.

Paste your photo or draw your picture here

My name is _____

_____ I am in Grade _____ and I study

at _____

HEY, IT'S ME! IT'S ME!

SUPER SKILLS

My three super skills are...

ACHIEVEMENT CORNER

My greatest achievements are...

LIFE GOALS

DREAM. BELIEVE. ACHIEVE

WHEN I GROW UP, I WANT TO BE
Illustrate the profession you want to be in when you're older.

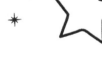

IN ORDER TO SUCCEED I MUST...
List down the three most important steps to achieve your goal.

HOW TO STAY ON TOP OF HOMEWORK

Staying on top of homework can be challenging, but some techniques can make it easier. Here are some tips for staying on top of homework:

- **Make a plan**: Set a schedule for your homework by making a to-do list or using a planner. This will help you stay organized and ensure you complete all assignments.

- **Get in the right mindset**: Find a quiet place to do your homework where you can focus without distractions. Put your phone on silent and take a break from social media while you work.

- **Take breaks**: Take short breaks to rest your mind and recharge your energy. Take a quick walk, listen to music, or grab a snack.

- **Break it up**: Break big assignments into smaller chunks. This will make them less overwhelming and easier to manage.

- **Get help**: If you're struggling with a particular assignment, feel free to ask for help. Reach out to your teacher or a tutor for extra support.

For example, if you have a big math test coming up, you can break it down by studying a little bit each day instead of trying to cram it all in the night before. Or, if you're having trouble focusing, you can take a short break every hour to stretch your legs and get some fresh air.

HOW TO USE A HOMEWORK TO-DO LIST AND PLANNER

A planner and to-do list are great tools for staying organized and on top of your tasks. Here's how you can use them to keep on top of your homework:

Firstly, create your to-do list:

- **Write down your tasks**: Write down all the homework you need to do every day.

- **Prioritize**: Look at your tasks and decide which ones are the most important or urgent. Mark these with a star or a different color.

- **Set deadlines**: For each task, set a deadline or due date.

Now use your planner:

- **Make a schedule**: Use your planner to schedule your work. This will help you stay organized and ensure you have enough time for everything.

- **Review and adjust**: Review your planner at the end of each day or week. Adjust your schedule as needed and move unfinished homework to the next day.

- **Use reminders**: set reminders on your phone or use sticky notes to remind you of deadlines or important tasks.

By using a to-do list and planner, you'll be better able to stay on top of your tasks and responsibilities and keep track of your progress. Remember to keep it simple and flexible and adjust it as needed.

Now it's your turn.

HOMEWORK TO-DO LIST

Every day write down all the things you need to do.

SUBJECT	TO-DO	DUE DATE

HOMEWORK PLANNER

Schedule your homework. Plot your to-dos in the space provided below. This will help you track your tasks and submit your homework and projects on time. Put a checkmark on each box once completed.

SUN	MON	TUE	WED	THU	FRI	SAT

CHAPTER 5

HEALTH
&
WELLNESS

Health and wellness are essential for our overall well-being. **Good physical and mental health can help us to feel happy, energized, and balanced.** It can also allow us to enjoy life more fully and make the most of our experiences.

In this chapter, we'll discuss how to maintain good physical and mental health. We'll look at how to practice healthy habits, how to stay safe and well-informed about our health, and how to get the support we need for our physical and mental health.

EXERCISE

Exercise is vital for everyone! When you exercise, your body moves, and your heart beats faster. This helps your muscles and bones get stronger, and it can also improve your mood and make you feel good.

Exercise is also a great way to manage stress and anxiety. When you exercise, your body produces chemicals called endorphins which can make you feel happier and more relaxed. Regular exercise can help reduce your stress and anxiety levels, which can help you feel better overall.

Additionally, exercise can help boost your energy levels, improve your sleep, and aid in maintaining a healthy weight. It can also make you feel better about your body, increasing your self-esteem and confidence.

There are many different types of exercise that you can do, and it's good to find something that you enjoy. Some examples include playing sports, riding a bike, swimming, or even dancing to your favorite music.

Making physical activity a regular part of your day is a great way to start. Try to do at least 30 minutes of exercise each day. This could be broken up into shorter bursts of activity. Even a few minutes of light activity, such as taking a walk or doing yoga stretches, can make you feel better.

Remember, a habit becomes a routine when you do it repeatedly. So, try to make exercise a regular part of your day!

HOME WORKOUT EXERCISES

You don't need a gym to get active. Here are some simple exercises you can do.

PLANK
Hold your body in a push-up position while engaging your stomach for one minute. Drop to your knees if you find it too difficult.

SQUATS
Stand with your feet shoulder-width apart and lower your hips back and down as if you were sitting into a chair. Keep your back straight.

TOE TOUCH
Stand with your feet wide apart. Bend down keeping your back straight and touch your left toe with your right hand. Swing and repeat to the right.

CRUNCHES
Lie on your back with your knees bent. Lift your shoulders off the floor towards your knees, keeping your lower back pressed to the floor.

LUNGES
Take a big step forward, bending both legs. Return to a standing position by pushing back up through the heel of the front foot.

HIGH KNEES
Run on the spot, lifting one knee at a time as high as possible towards your chest. Try to do this for 60 seconds.

SIDE PLANK
Lie on one side & prop yourself up on one elbow, keeping your legs straight, core engaged and hold for 30 seconds. Repeat on the other side.

CYCLING
If you can, ask your parents or an adult to take you for a cycle ride.

EXERCISE
ACTIVITY LOG

Remember, a habit becomes a routine when you do it repeatedly. Mark off the days you exercise and include the total number of minutes you do each day.

SUN	MON	TUE	WED	THU	FRI	SAT

EXERCISE
ACHIEVEMENTS

Great job! Here are your achievement badges for completing various exercises. To stay motivated, mark them off when you achieve them.

☐ **Getting Started!**

Great job, you've done your first workout!

☐ **Walking Wonder**

Good work, you walked 3 miles in a day!

☐ **Fitness Fanatic**

You're on a winning streak - 5 days in a row!

☐ **Strength Squad**

Awesome, you hit 50 push-ups in one day!

☐ **Cardio Champ**

Nice. You just ran in your first race!

☐ **Jump for Joy**

Lookin' good. 100 jumping jacks in a row!

☐ **Healthy Hero**

Well done, you're winning streak is up to 10 days!

☐ **Exercise MVP**

Good work, you exercised for 50 consecutive days!

☐ **Fit Boss 100**

You did it! You've exercised for 100 consecutive days!

RECREATIONAL ACTIVITIES

Find all the recreational activities and circle them. List the words you found below. Clue: There are nine activities.

```
R H T Y O G A Q D V
I W I F W N R B S O
S W I M M I N G S L
I A Y A Z F A L E L
G N I K K E R T H E
O E Y E P C N M C Y
L L A B T E K S A B
F E J U Y X R H N A
J O G G I N G O J L
G N I C N A D S S L
```

1._____   4._____   7._____

2._____   5._____   8._____

3._____   6._____   9._____

HEALTHY EATING

Healthy eating is an integral part of overall health. Eating a balanced diet can help you to feel your best and gives you the energy your body needs to grow, learn and play.

Think of your body like an engine.

Just like an engine needs the right fuel to run well, your body needs the right food to function well. If you put the wrong fuel in your car's engine, it won't run well, and if you eat the wrong kind of food, your body won't function well either.

Eating healthy foods like fruits, vegetables, whole grains, lean proteins, and low-fat dairy is like putting premium gas in your car's engine. It runs smoothly and efficiently. These foods give your body the nutrients it needs to grow and stay healthy.

But, when you overeat junk food, like candy, cookies, and fried foods, it's like putting cheap, low-quality fuel in your car's engine. It may run, but not as well, and can lead to damage over time. These foods are high in sugar, fat, and calories and do not provide your body with the essential nutrients it needs to grow and thrive.

Just like how you take care of your car's engine by regularly changing the oil and having it serviced, you also need to take care of your body's engine by feeding it healthy foods and exercising regularly.

HEALTHY VS. UNHEALTHY FOOD

Healthy eating starts by making better food choices. Write a list or draw some foods that are healthy on the left & unhealthy on the right.

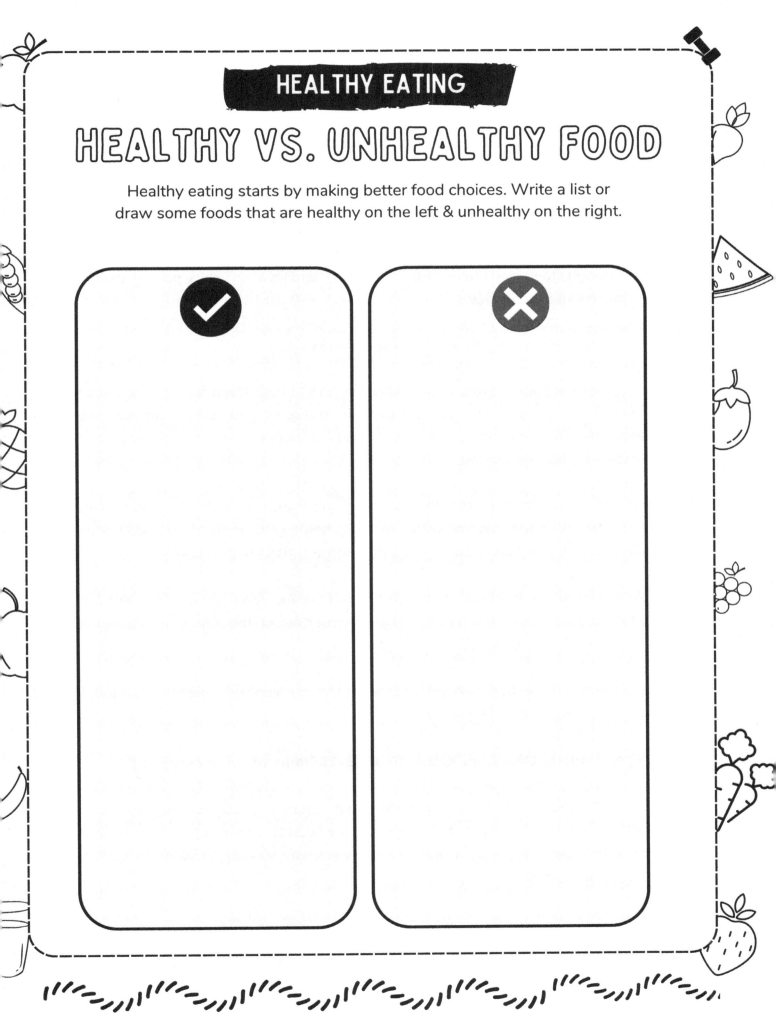

SLEEP

Sleep is your secret superpower! When you get a good night's sleep, you wake up feeling refreshed and ready to take on the day. But when you don't get enough sleep, you may feel tired, grumpy, and have difficulty paying attention in school or activities.

Just like how superheroes have special powers to help them fight crime and save the day, sleep gives you superpowers too! **Sleep allows your body and brain to grow and repair.** It also enables you to learn and remember new things, so you can excel in school and other activities.

During sleep, your brain sorts through information and memories from the day and helps you learn and retain new information. It also helps with creativity and problem-solving skills, so you can develop new ideas and find solutions to problems.

Sleep also helps to boost your immune system, meaning you are less likely to catch a cold or get sick. It also helps to regulate your mood and emotions, making you feel happier and less stressed.

Just like how superheroes need to recharge their powers, you need to get enough sleep to rejuvenate your body and brain.

A good rule of thumb for kids is to get 9-11 hours of sleep every night.

So, go to bed at a regular time every night, create a peaceful sleeping environment and make sure to disconnect from screens for at least 1 hour before bed. By doing this, you'll be sure to wake up feeling like the superhero you are, ready to tackle whatever the day throws at you!

IMPROVE YOUR SLEEP

Sleep is your secret super power! Have a look through the tips below to help recharge your powers!

- Create a relaxing evening routine every night.
- Go to bed at the same time each night.
- Read a book before going to bed.
- Take a relaxing bath.
- Avoid screens in the hour before bedtime.
- Create a calm environment in your bedroom: Dark, quiet, cool.
- Ensure you get enough fresh air, sunlight, and exercise during the day.
- Avoid sleeping with a full stomach.

SCREENTIME

Screens can be an enjoyable way to stay connected with friends and family, watch movies, play games, create art, and explore the world in a few clicks.

However, screen time can have a negative impact on your health and well-being. Spending too much time on screens can lead to a sedentary lifestyle, harming your physical health. Additionally, too much screentime can lead to eye strains and headaches and affect sleep.

It's good to limit your time on screens each day and take breaks if necessary. Try to balance your daily activities so that you have a mix of things that are good for your body and mind, like playing sports, reading, and spending time with friends and family.

There are many things you can do to limit your screen time.

Set a timer

Use apps to limit access

Schedule specific times for you to be on screens

If you spend too much time on a screen, start by limiting your time on each device and setting a timer for yourself. You might find it helpful to write a promise to yourself on paper to remind you of your goal.

SCREENTIME

PROMISE TO MYSELF

CONTRACT AGREEMENT

I _____ promise to abide by the following rules regarding screen time.

I will have this much total screen time in a

Day _____
Week _____

- ☐ Screen time will never get in the way of my homework.
- ☐ When my screen time is over, I will stop it without an argument.
- ☐ Screen time will never get in the way of household chores.
- ☐ I understand that some days I may only get some of my screen time (if I have other obligations during the day).

_____   _____
Name & Signature   Date

CHAPTER 6

MONEY MATTERS

> Money is an essential part of our daily lives. It helps us buy the things we need and want, like food, clothes, and toys. But it's important to understand that money doesn't grow on trees, and we must work to earn it.

When you start earning money, whether it's from allowance, doing chores, or a part-time job, it's important to learn how to manage it well. This means setting goals for how to spend it, saving a portion of it, and learning to budget. This helps ensure you always have enough money to buy the things you need and reach your long-term goals, such as buying a new bike.

In this chapter, you'll learn:

- The basics of money, such as earning and spending it.
- How to set financial goals and budget your money.
- Different types of money, such as cash, debit cards, credit cards, and online banking.

The basics of money

Learning the basics of money is vital for future financial success. Here are a few key terms to help you get started:

- **Earnings** are money you earn from allowance, chores, or a part-time job.
- **Spending** refers to how you use your earnings to buy things you need and want.
- **Saving** is putting aside a portion of your earnings to reach long-term goals.
- **Budgeting** refers to planning and managing your spending to meet short-term and long-term goals.

By understanding these basic concepts, you can make informed decisions about how to use your money responsibly.

BUDGETING

Budgeting is a way to plan how you spend and save money.

It's like making a plan for your money, so you know exactly where it's going and can ensure you have enough for the things you need and want.

One way to budget is to list everything you want to spend money on, like clothes, toys, or video games. Next, consider how much money you have available and divide it among the things on your list. This way, you can see how much money you have for each item and can make sure you spend your money wisely.

MONEY TRACKER

Tracking your expenses gives you a better understanding of where your money is going. Write down every time you spend money in a week.

MONTHLY EXPENSES TRACKER

Date	Item	Amount
Total		

WHERE DOES YOUR MONEY GO?

Create a pie chart in the circle, splitting your spending by the categories.

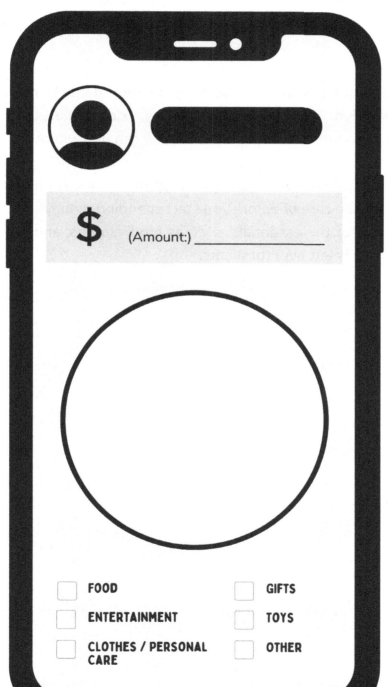

$ (Amount:) _____

☐ **FOOD**

☐ **ENTERTAINMENT**

☐ **CLOTHES / PERSONAL CARE**

☐ **GIFTS**

☐ **TOYS**

☐ **OTHER**

Spending money wisely — Wants vs. Needs

When spending money, it's essential to understand the difference between wants and needs.

A need is something you have to have, like food, shelter, and clothes. These are things that you can't live without and that you should always budget for. *For example, you need to buy groceries every week, you need clothes to wear, and you need a place to live.*

On the other hand, a want is something you would like to have but don't necessarily need to survive. This can include new toys, video games, or the latest phone. These are things that you would like to have but you can live without.

When making a budget or planning your spending, focus on your needs first and ensure they are taken care of before you start spending money on wants. This means you need to budget for the essentials, such as food, clothes, and a place to live, and then see what money is left over for wants.

BUDGETING

WANTS VS. NEEDS

In each separate box, illustrate below the possible needs and wants of young people.

NEEDS

A need is something you have to have, like food, shelter, and clothes.

WANTS

A want is something you would like to have, but that you don't need to survive, like new toys, video games, or the latest phone.

SAVINGS & SETTING FINANCIAL GOALS

Setting financial goals is also an essential part of budgeting. It means thinking about what you want to save for in the future, like a new bike or video game. Once you have set your goal, you can start planning how to save up for it. One way to do this is by setting aside a certain amount from your allowance or earnings each week or month.

It's important to remember that saving for a big goal takes time, so you must be patient and consistent with saving. Keep track of your savings in a piggy bank or a special savings account at the bank, so you can see how much you've saved and how close you are to reach your goal.

By understanding these basic concepts, you can make informed decisions about how to use your money responsibly.

SAVINGS GOAL PLANNER

Think about what you want to save for in the future, like a new bike or video game. Mark down every time you set aside some money from your allowance or earnings each week or month.

SAVING FOR : _____

AMOUNT : _____   **DUE BY :** _____

TOTAL :

NOTES : _____

_____

DIFFERENT TYPES OF MONEY

Money is money, right? Well, not necessarily. There are several different types of money, and it's helpful to understand their differences.

- **Cash**: Cash is physical money, like paper bills and coins, that you can hold and use to buy things. It is widely accepted and does not require more information than the amount.

- **Debit Card**: A debit card is linked to a checking or savings account and can be used to make purchases or withdraw cash from an ATM. The money is deducted directly from your account balance when you use a debit card.

- **Credit Card**: A credit card allows you to borrow money from a bank to make purchases. You'll be required to pay back the borrowed amount and interest. Credit cards also allow you to build a credit history if you pay your balance on time.

- **Buy Now Pay Later**: Some stores offer plans that allow you to make a purchase now and pay for it later, usually with interest. They can be a way to buy something you might not have the money for yet, but it's important to understand the terms and make sure you can afford the payments.

- **Online Banking**: This refers to banking through the internet, where you can check your account balance, pay bills, transfer money, and more. This allows you to access your money and bank account information from anywhere.

It's important to remember that all these types of money have their own benefits and drawbacks, and it's essential to use them responsibly and understand the terms and conditions before using them.

PAYMENT METHODS

List the possible pros & cons of the different types of payment methods.

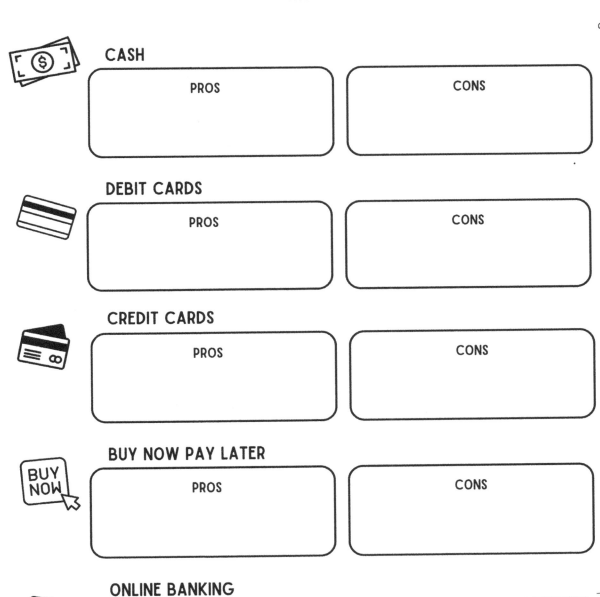

CASH

PROS	CONS

DEBIT CARDS

PROS	CONS

CREDIT CARDS

PROS	CONS

BUY NOW PAY LATER

PROS	CONS

ONLINE BANKING

PROS	CONS

CHAPTER 7

COOKING SKILLS

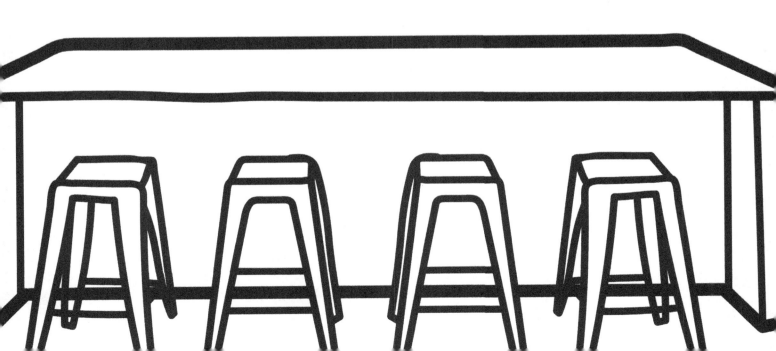

Cooking is a valuable skill to learn, not only for practical reasons but also because it can help you stay healthy and save money. Learning how to cook your own meals at home can be an empowering experience as you gain confidence in the kitchen and become more independent. You'll also know different foods better, understand flavors, and develop your palate.

Cooking is also a great way to get creative! You can experiment with different recipes and ingredients, discover new flavors, and let your imagination run wild.

Learning to cook is a skill that will benefit you in many ways, so take the time to practice and get comfortable with cooking. Once you have the basics down, you can explore different recipes and ingredients, expand your flavor horizons, and even impress your friends with delicious home-cooked meals. So don't be afraid to jump in the kitchen — cooking can be an enjoyable and rewarding skill with some practice.

ESSENTIAL ITEMS

Before you start cooking, you must ensure you have all the necessary tools and ingredients.

- **Pots, pans, and other necessary cookware**: These are essential for cooking on the stovetop or in the oven.

- **Utensils**: Spoons, spatulas, tongs, and other tools will help stir, flip, and move food around as needed.

- **Ingredients**: Ensure you have the ingredients for the recipe you're making, including pantry staples like salt, pepper, and oil.

- **A cutting board**: This will be handy for chopping and slicing fruits, vegetables, and other ingredients.

- **Knives**: Having a variety of knives (like paring knives, chef's knives, and serrated knives) will make prepping ingredients much easier.

Once you have these tools, you're ready to start cooking!

Work through the activities on the following few pages, and try some delicious recipes yourself! Good luck!

INGREDIENTS & COOKING EQUIPMENT

Illustrate equipment & ingredients you might need to cook.

READY, SET, COOK!

How well do you know the kitchen? Draw a circle around the spices, put a box around the cooking tools, and mark an (×) next to everything else.

COOKING METHODS

How well do you know your cooking methods?

Identify the following cooking methods:

SAUTÉ   SIMMER   STEAM

GRILL   ROAST   BOIL

RECIPES

READING RECIPES

Read the recipe and answer the questions below.

Taco Recipe

Ingredients:
- 1 lb ground beef
- **2** tablespoons taco seasoning
- **8** soft tacos shells or hard taco shells
- Shredded lettuce, diced tomatoes, shredded cheese, sour cream (optional)

Instructions:
1. In a large skillet over medium heat, cook the ground beef until it is no longer pink.
2. Add the taco seasoning and cook for an additional 1-2 minutes until the seasoning has blended into the beef.
3. Place **2-3** tablespoons of seasoned beef in each taco shell.
4. Top with lettuce, tomatoes, cheese, and sour cream (optional).
5. Serve and enjoy!

To make a vegetarian alternative, swap ground beef for a plant-based protein, such as black beans or quinoa.

----

1. What type of skillet is best to use when cooking ground beef?

2. How much taco seasoning should you add to the beef?

3. Can you use hard taco shells instead of using soft tacos?

4. Are there any other toppings you could add to the tacos?

5. How could you make this vegetarian?

LET'S COOK

DISH OF THE DAY!

Imagine you are a chef and you recently opened a restaurant; use your imagination to create a dish of the day! Here is an example recipe.

Draw your dish

NAME YOUR DISH:

Eggs en cocotte de Monica

DESCRIBE YOUR DISH:

Scrambled eggs with my very own twist. I added my special mix of spices and something else to make it fluffy and soft.

MATERIALS:

Frying pan   Knife
Frying ladle   Cutting board
Plate
Whisk
Bowl
Fork

INGREDIENTS:

6 eggs   Baking Powder

1/4 cup milk   special spices mix

Onions (finely chopped)

1 tablespoon butter

INSTRUCTIONS:

1. Crack the eggs into a bowl and whisk together with the milk.
2. Melt the butter in a frying pan over medium heat.
3. Pour in the eggs and cook, stirring occasionally, until they are set.
4. Season with salt and pepper to taste.
5. Serve hot with toast or on a bed of greens.

CHEF'S SIGNATURE

YOUR TURN!

DISH OF THE DAY!

Imagine you are a chef and you recently opened a restaurant; use your imagination to create a dish of the day!

Draw your dish

NAME YOUR DISH:

DESCRIBE YOUR DISH:

MATERIALS:

INGREDIENTS:

INSTRUCTIONS:

CHEF'S SIGNATURE

CHAPTER 8

HAPPINESS SKILLS

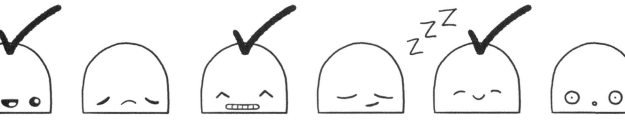

Do you ever get that warm, fuzzy feeling when you spend time with your friends and family or when you accomplish something you've been working hard on?

That's happiness.

Happiness is like a big smile that spreads across your face and makes you feel good inside. It's that feeling that makes you feel like you're on top of the world.

Happiness is also a state of mind; it's a mindset you can choose. It's about looking at the positive things in your life and being grateful for them rather than focusing on the negative.

In short, happiness is a feeling of being content, satisfied, and fulfilled. It's a beautiful feeling that can bring a sense of peace and well-being. It's something that you can choose to experience by focusing on the positive things in your life, spending time with people you love, taking care of your body, and being kind to others.

The good news is that happiness is a skill that can be learned, just like learning to cook or ride a bike. In this chapter, we'll explore things you can do to help boost your mood.

THINGS THAT MAKE ME HAPPY

What makes you happy? Think about the question and write or draw in the boxes below things that put a smile on your face and make you feel good inside.

WHAT IS YOUR PERFECT DAY?

How would you describe your perfect day? Use the space below and draw what your perfect day would look like. Here are some prompts to help you get started:

Where will you spend your perfect day?

Who are you with or are you alone?

What would you do?

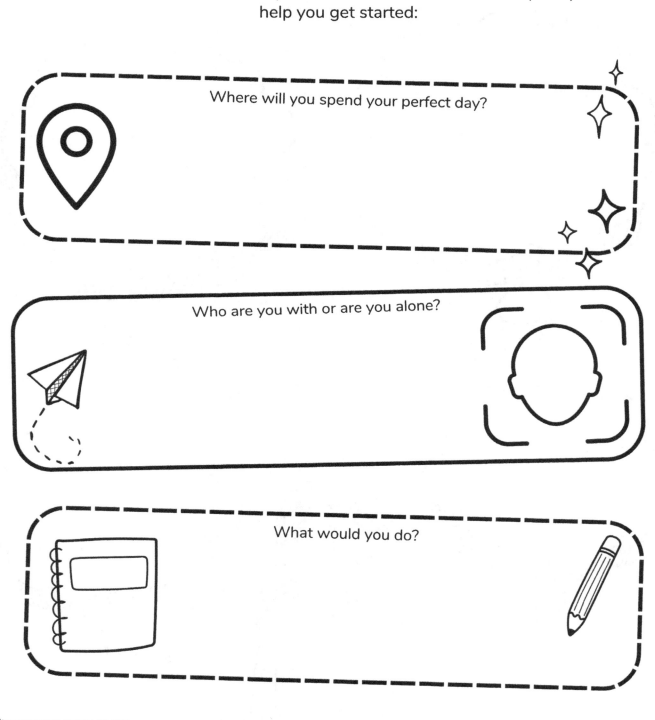

FINDING THINGS YOU'RE GOOD AT

Happiness is closely linked to feeling a sense of accomplishment, so it's important to identify things you're good at and nurture them. It could be anything from painting and drawing to playing an instrument or coding. Spend some time trying out different activities and see what resonates with you. You may find something you didn't even know you were good at!

Once you know what you enjoy, make time for those activities and challenge yourself. Doing something that makes you proud of your accomplishments will bring joy to your life — so go for it!

Doing things you enjoy

Life isn't all about work and obligations; it's also essential to do what you enjoy. Whether playing a board game with your family, watching a movie, or exploring nature — make sure to set aside time for activities that bring you joy.

These activities will help give you some balance in life and can even help to reduce stress levels. So don't be afraid to take a break from your daily routine and do something special just for yourself!

FINDING YOUR HAPPY PLACE

Everyone has a "Happy Place" — a place or activity that helps them relax and rejuvenate. Maybe it's sitting by the ocean, walking in the park, or watching a favorite show. Whatever makes you feel relaxed and content — that's your happy place!

Make sure to take the time to visit it whenever you're feeling overwhelmed or need a break from life. You'll be surprised how much peace and comfort you can find there.

# HOW TO FIND THINGS YOU'RE GOOD AT

Happiness is linked to feeling a sense of accomplishment, so it's important to identify things you're good at. Start by identifying the things you enjoy doing. If you enjoy doing something, chances are you'll be good at it or become good at it.

 **THINGS I ENJOY...**

THINGS I DON'T ENJOY...

FIND YOUR HAPPY PLACE...

Everyone has a "Happy Place." Take some time to think about what makes you happy. Close your eyes and try to visualize your happy place, then answer the questions below.

What do you see?

What can you feel or touch?

What can you smell or taste?

How do you feel?

What do you hear?

STAYING POSITIVE

Positive thinking is another way to increase happiness. **It's about seeing the good in situations, focusing on the things that bring you joy, and training yourself to think more optimistically.**

Having a positive attitude also helps build better relationships with others. When you're positive, you're more likely to be kind and compassionate, which helps you connect with others and form strong, healthy relationships.

Moreover, positivity also positively impacts our physical and mental health. Studies have shown that people with a positive outlook tend to have lower stress levels, improved immune function, and better overall physical health. They also tend to be less prone to depression and anxiety.

POSITIVITY!

Design a phone case, bottle & cap using colorful, positive-thinking messages and designs. You may find the words & phrases below helpful.

CERTIFIED HAPPY

HELPFUL WORDS & PHRASES

- You can do it!
- Never give up!
- I'm awesome!
- Happy
- Kind
- Friendly
- Strong
- Brave
- Creative
- Joy

MY "FEEL-GOOD" PLAYLIST

Choose happiness all the time! Listening to certain types of music can create positive emotions such as happiness, excitement, and contentment. Create your own "Feel-Good" playlist below. Draw an album cover for your playlist!

SHOWING GRATITUDE

Showing gratitude to the people and things in your life is a great way to find happiness. It can help you recognize how much you have, even if it isn't perfect. Taking time to appreciate what we have — whether it's material possessions or relationships — can bring joy and contentment into our lives.

Moreover, having an attitude of gratitude can also help us stay humble and practice empathy. We become more aware of other people's needs, and we're better able to appreciate our successes in life.

Take the time each day to think about what you're grateful for — it's a powerful way to increase happiness!

CHAPTER 9

CARING
&
SHARING

Caring and sharing are essential life skills everyone should learn. When we are kind and generous, we build stronger relationships and make the world a better place. Additionally, it helps us appreciate the world around us and our role in it.

Caring for animals is a great way to develop caring skills. When you take care of a pet, you learn about responsibility and how to care for others. You can also volunteer at a local animal shelter and help take care of animals that need a home. By caring for animals, you learn about empathy and compassion, which are valuable skills to have in life.

Caring for the environment is also important. It helps to preserve the earth and all the living things that depend on it. You can do this by recycling, conserving water and energy, and reducing waste. Every little bit helps, and you'll feel good knowing you're doing your part to care for the planet.

Caring for your family is also crucial. By helping out with household chores, being kind and supportive, and spending quality time together, you can develop strong bonds with your family members and learn how to care for others.

In this chapter, you'll find some worksheets to help you learn more about the power of caring and sharing. You'll discover how a small act of kindness can make a big difference in someone's life and how you can use your talents to give back to your community. So get ready for some fun activities that will teach you all about the importance of caring and sharing!

CARING FOR THE ENVIRONMENT

Did you know that if every American household replaced just one roll of paper towels with reusable cloth towels, we could save 544,000 trees each year!

That's the power of collective action. Every person's actions, big or small, make a difference. It may not seem like much, but collectively, small changes can have a considerable impact.

By taking small actions daily, you can make a big difference in caring for the environment and preserving it for future generations.

Here are just a few things that you can do:

- **Reduce, Reuse, Recycle**: One of the best ways to care for the environment is to reduce the amount of waste you produce. Instead of buying new things, try to find ways to reuse items you already have. When you can't reuse something, recycle it instead of throwing it away.

- **Conserve Energy**: Another way to care for the environment is to conserve energy. This can be as simple as turning off lights and electronics when you're not using them or unplugging chargers when they're not in use.

- **Plant Trees**: Planting trees is one of the most effective ways to absorb carbon dioxide from the atmosphere, which helps to reduce the effects of climate change.

- **Use public transportation**: Walking, biking, or using public transportation instead of driving can also help reduce your carbon footprint and pollution.

- **Save water**: Water is a precious resource, and one of the most important things you can do to care for the environment is to save water. You can do this by turning off the faucet when you're brushing your teeth or taking shorter showers.

- **Be mindful of the products you buy**: Try to select eco-friendly products that are sustainably produced.

Remember, every little bit helps, and it is essential to do what you can when you can.

CARING FOR THE
ENVIRONMENT

What are some ways you could care for the environment at home
and in school - e.g. turning off lights, recycling, etc.

*action*plan

HOME

- _____
- _____
- _____
- _____

SCHOOL

- _____
- _____
- _____
- _____

¡ SAVE
EARTH !

RECYCLE, REUSE, REFUSE

You can do many things to help care for the planet, like recycling, reusing, and refusing. Add the items below.

ITEMS I CAN RECYCLE

ITEMS I CAN REFUSE

ITEMS I CAN REUSE

SAY NO to PLASTIC

SHOWING KINDNESS & CARING FOR YOUR COMMUNITY

Caring for your community and showing kindness to others is just as important as caring for the environment. It helps to build a sense of belonging, make a positive impact on the lives of others, and set an example for others to follow. Small actions can make a big difference, so even if you're only able to do a little bit, it still counts.

Did you know that helping others and showing kindness can also improve your mental health? Studies have shown that people who engage in acts of kindness are more likely to feel happier and less stressed.

Here are some examples of ways that you can show care for the community and kindness to others:

- **Volunteer**: One of the best ways to show care for the community is to volunteer your time. You can help at a local food bank, participate in a clean-up effort, or assist at a community center.

- **Help a neighbor**: Simple acts, such as helping a neighbor in need, can make a big difference. Offer to run an errand for an elderly neighbor or shovel the sidewalk for a family with small children.

- **Show empathy**: Showing interest in what others are going through and offering a kind word or gesture can make a huge difference in someone's day. This can be as simple as smiling at someone having a tough day.

- **Give back**: This can be done by volunteering at a local charity, donating clothes or other items to those in need, or making a monetary donation to a cause you believe in.

- **Support local businesses**: Supporting local businesses helps boost the local economy and promotes the community and its people.

For example, if you see someone struggling with a heavy load, you can offer to help them carry it. Or, you can volunteer at a homeless shelter or soup kitchen to provide meals for people in need.

You can positively impact your community and the people around you by taking small actions daily.

CARING FOR YOUR COMMUNITY

What can you do to help make your neighborhood a better place to live? List some positive actions (like helping your neighbor with their shopping) and negative actions (like littering).

Positive Actions

Negative Actions

KINDNESS CALENDAR

	WEEK 1	WEEK 2	WEEK 3
MON	Give someone a gift	Eat a meal together	Do chores at home
TUE	Listen to a friend's problem	Give an unexpected compliment	Stop to assist someone who looks lost
WED	Help someone with their work	Donate unwanted toys or old books	Make new friends
THU	hello — Say good morning to someone	Tell your family how much you love them	Help an elderly person
FRI	Open a door for someone	You're awesome! — Leave a nice note on a mirror	THANK YOU — Write a thank you note to a family member
SAT	Hug someone you love	Give up your seat to someone	Donate items to a charity
SUN	Share with someone	Write a thank you note to your friends	Play with animals at a local shelter

CHAPTER 10

COMMUNICATION SKILLS

Communication skills are crucial life skills for young adults! **Effective communication lets you express your thoughts, opinions, and feelings clearly so that people understand where you're coming from.**

Think of communication skills as a superpower. Whenever you find yourself in a difficult situation, communicating confidently and effectively can help you navigate it successfully.

For example, if you're having trouble understanding your math homework, communicating with your teacher or tutor can help you figure out the problem.

On the other hand, if you're feeling down or angry about something, talking to a trusted friend can help you work through your feelings and make sense of them.

In this chapter, we'll cover the basics of communication and how to develop these skills so that you can communicate effectively with everyone in your life. From having conversations to writing thank you letters, we'll discuss all the different ways to get your point across! So get ready for fun activities that will help you become a master communicator and make strong connections with others.

The different types of communication
But first up. What exactly are communication skills?

Communication skills are the abilities and techniques that allow us to effectively convey our thoughts, feelings, and ideas to others.

They include a variety of different skills, such as:

- **Listening**: The ability to pay attention to and understand what someone else is saying.

- **Verbal communication**: The ability to express ourselves using spoken language, including tone of voice, word choice, and grammar.

- **Nonverbal communication**: The ability to communicate using body language, facial expressions, and other nonverbal cues.

- **Writing**: The ability to express ourselves using written language, including spelling, grammar, and organization.

- **Conflict resolution**: The ability to handle disagreements and conflicts constructively and effectively.

- **Empathy**: The ability to understand and share the feelings of others.

All these skills are essential to master to communicate effectively with others.

LISTENING

Learning to listen effectively is one of the most critical communication skills. **Through active listening, you can understand what someone else is saying and show that you care about their thoughts and feelings.**

Some techniques for effective listening include:

- **Paying attention** to what is being said.
- **Asking questions** to clarify any misunderstandings.
- **Refraining from distractions** such as phones, computers, etc.
- **Not interrupting** or jumping to conclusions.
- **Taking notes** so that you can remember every point.

By practicing these techniques, you'll develop your listening skills and be able to understand and empathize with others more effectively.

ACTIVE LISTENING

Active listening is paying close attention to what someone is saying and responding in a way that shows you understand them. Color in the shapes that describe active listening.

NODDING YOUR HEAD

ASKING QUESTIONS

CHECKING YOUR PHONE

INTERRUPTING

MAKING EYE CONTACT

REMEMBERING DETAILS

YAWNING

LOOKING AROUND

SMILING

CHECKING YOUR WATCH

LETTING THE OTHER FINISH

VERBAL COMMUNICATION

Communicating using spoken language is an essential skill for any age. **Verbal communication includes tone of voice, word choice, and grammar.**

It's necessary to practice these skills to communicate effectively, especially in difficult conversations.

Some tips for effective verbal communication include:

- **Speaking clearly** and using the right words to convey your message.
- **Using appropriate body language**, such as eye contact and open posture.
- **Taking turns during a conversation** and allowing others to have their say.
- **Being mindful of tone and volume** so you don't come across as too aggressive or intimidating.
- **Avoiding using words like "should" and "must"** because they can be perceived as bossy or demanding.

By practicing these techniques, you'll be able to communicate more effectively and confidently with others.

NONVERBAL COMMUNICATION

Nonverbal communication is the way we communicate without using words. It includes things like body language, facial expressions, and gestures. Being able to understand and interpret nonverbal cues is essential for effective communication.

Some tips for being aware of nonverbal cues include:

- Observing others' body language, facial expressions, and gestures.
- Understanding the subtle differences between facial expressions like a smile or frown.
- Noticing when someone isn't comfortable or engaged in a conversation.
- Paying attention to how someone's tone of voice changes during a conversation.

By being aware of these cues, you'll be able to better understand the feelings and intentions of others.

BODY LANGUAGE

Body language can convey positive and negative messages to others. Take a look at the gestures below. Describe them and decide if they are positive or negative.

WRITING

Being able to express yourself in writing is a skill everyone has to learn. **Writing involves things like spelling, grammar, and organization.** It's essential to practice these skills to communicate effectively with others through written communication.

Some tips for effective writing include:

- **Brainstorm ideas** before you start writing.

- **Organize your thoughts** in a logical order, so they're easy to follow.

- **Be aware of the tone** and audience of your writing.

- **Check for typos** and spelling mistakes before submitting your work.

By practicing these techniques, you'll be able to write more clearly and confidently.

HOW CAN I HELP YOU?

Using live chat can be a great way to ask for help and get the information you need quickly and easily. Read through the example below to see how you might use chat.

SCENARIO

You ordered a new video game from an online store, but when you received it, it wouldn't work on your gaming console.

Note: It's always helpful to be specific and provide all the necessary information when asking for help with a problem you're having with a product you bought online, it helps to resolve the problem efficiently.

Below is an imagined conversation with the customer service agent.

Hi, this is Jane, how can i help you today?

Hi, I recently purchased a video game from you, but it's not working on my console.

Sorry to hear that. Can you please provide your order number and the specific error message you're receiving?

Sure, the order number is ABC456 and the error message says "disc read error".

Thanks, it sounds like there may be a problem with the disc. I'll process a replacement to be sent out to you.

Thanks so much, appreciate your help.

HOW CAN I HELP YOU?

Now it's your turn. Read through the scenario and imagine how you might solve the problem.

SCENARIO

You bought a new t-shirt from an online store, but when you tried it on, it was too small. You'd like to exchange it for a larger size or get a refund.

Fill in the blank bubbles to solve the problem.

HI, THIS IS JOHN, HOW CAN I HELP YOU TODAY?

THANK YOU LETTER

There are many reasons to be grateful. For this activity, write a thank you letter to your favorite person.

CHAPTER 11

PRACTICAL SKILLS

Learning practical skills is essential for young people as they transition into adulthood. **Not only do they help you take care of yourself and become independent, but they also give you the confidence to take on new challenges and make you feel more secure in your own abilities.**

Think about it like this: When you know how to clean your room, you'll have a clean and organized space to relax. When you know how to use a washing machine, you'll be able to do your own laundry without relying on anyone else. And when you know how to read a bus timetable, you'll be able to get around on your own and be more independent.

In this chapter of the workbook, you'll find practical activities that will support you in learning various life skills, from how to do your own laundry to changing a bike tire and read bus timetables.

It's good to be prepared for anything! With practice, you'll feel confident and capable of taking on challenges. Let's get started! Good luck!

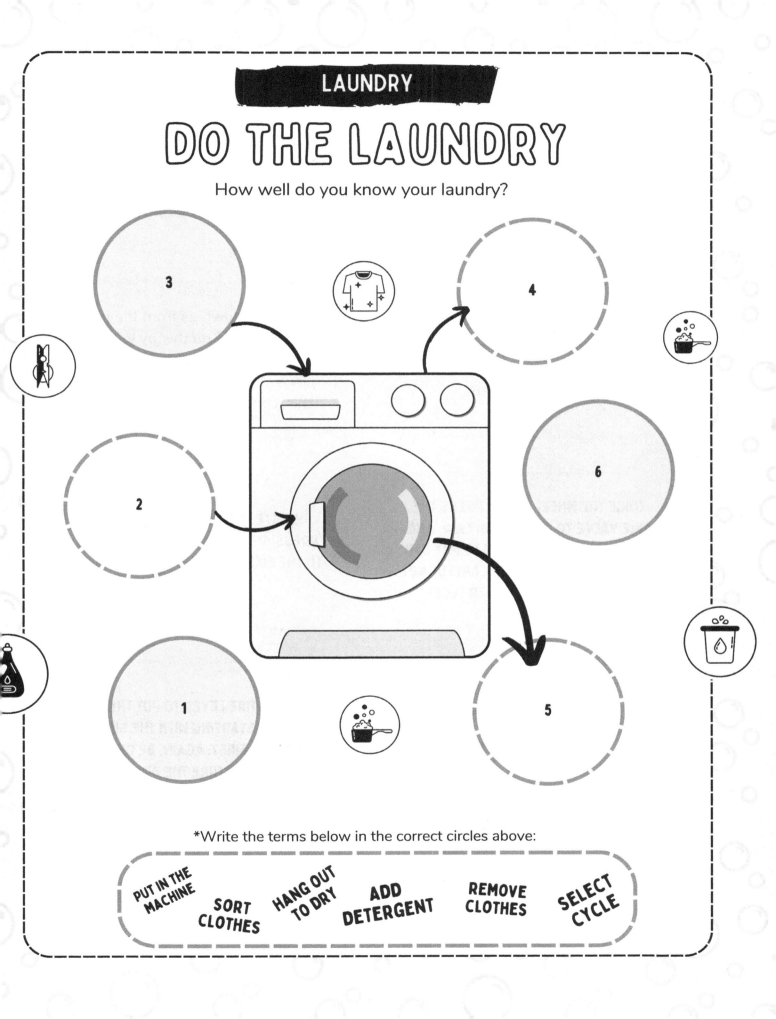

CHANGING A BIKE TIRE

How do you change a bike tire? Put the following steps in order using numbers 1-6.

○ REMOVE THE INNER TUBE ENTIRELY AND INSPECT IT FOR ANY HOLES OR PUNCTURES. IF YOU FIND A HOLE, YOU CAN TRY TO PATCH IT WITH A PATCH KIT.

○ Remove the wheel from the bike. You can usually do this by loosening the bolts that hold the wheel in place. If you're unsure how to do this, consult your bike's manual.

○ ONCE THE WHEEL IS OFF, PRESS THE TIRE VALVE TO REMOVE ANY AIR, AND THEN USE THE TIRE LEVER TO PRY OFF ONE SIDE OF THE TIRE. BE CAREFUL NOT TO PUNCTURE THE INNER TUBE!

○ INFLATE THE TIRE TO THE CORRECT PRESSURE AND REATTACH THE WHEEL TO THE BIKE. YOU'RE NOW READY TO HIT THE ROAD!

○ Inflate the new inner tube slightly and fit it inside the tire. Make sure it's not twisted.

○ USE THE TIRE LEVER TO PUT THE TIRE BACK ON, STARTING WITH THE SIDE YOU REMOVED FIRST. AGAIN, BE CAREFUL NOT TO PUNCTURE THE INNER TUBE.

READING A BUS TIMETABLE

BUS TIMETABLE

FROM ST. PAUL'S CATHEDRAL TO BUCKINGHAM PALACE   FREE BUS RIDE

BUS STOPS	DAY TIMES						
ST. PAUL'S CATHEDRAL	08:34	10:12	11:45	13:45	14:30	16:30	18:45
TOWER OF LONDON	08:46	10:14	11:57	13:57	14:34	16:42	18:48
THE SHARD	08:48	10:22	11:59	13:59	14:42	16:44	18:50
TATE MODERN	08:56	10:29	12:14	14:07	14:44	16:52	18:58
LONDON EYE	09:03	10:38	12:23	14:14	14:52	16:59	19:05
WESTMINSTER	09:12	10:43	12:28	14:23	14:53	17:04	19:14
DOWNING STREET	09:17	10:49	12:34	14:28	15:08	17:13	19:19
OXFORD CIRCUS	09:30	10:56	12:41	14:34	15:15	17:19	19:25
BUCKINGHAM PALACE	09:38	11:04	12:49	14:41	15:19	17:26	19:32

ACTIVITY TIME!

Read the bus timetable above to answer the questions below.

1   Which stop is after Westminster?

2   Jim is catching the 18.45 bus from St. Paul's to the London Eye. How long will he be on the bus for?

3   Jane is at The Shard, and needs to get to Oxford Circus before 15.00. Which bus must she get to arrive in time?

CHAPTER 12

PERSONAL SAFETY

Personal safety is an essential aspect of life that helps protect us from harm and danger.

In this chapter of the workbook, you'll find activities that will teach you about personal safety and provide tips and strategies for staying safe in different situations. It includes topics such as internet safety, spotting fake news and recognizing scams, and tips for when you're out in public.

Before we go into the individual topics, there are a few overarching safety rules to remember:

- Pay attention to your surroundings.
- Trust your instincts and be aware of any warning signs.
- Plan ahead for potential dangers.
- Know how to contact help if needed.

Now let's dive into the details of staying safe in your everyday life!

USING PUBLIC TRANSPORT SAFELY

Staying safe on public transport is vital at any age. Whether commuting to school or just taking a trip, it's important to know how to stay safe using buses, trains, and subways.

Public transport is usually a convenient and efficient way to travel, but it can also be crowded, noisy, and chaotic. By following these safety tips, you can enjoy your journey and arrive at your destination safely.

STAYING SAFE
ON PUBLIC TRANSPORT

✓ DO'S

- Plan your route in advance.

- Tell a family member or friend about your travel plans.

- If possible, travel with a friend or family member when using public transport.

- Go to well-lit areas if you are travelling at night.

- Trust your intuition—if you feel uneasy, leave the area.

- Know the emergency exits, and carry a charged phone with emergency contact numbers.

- Stand back from the edge of the platform while waiting for the train or bus.

✕ DON'TS

- Don't block the aisles or doorways.

- Don't distract the driver or operator, they need to focus on the road or tracks.

- Avoid taking a call, talking loudly or listening to loud music.

- Don't litter or vandalize public transport.

- Avoid travelling alone late at night and in unfamiliar areas.

- Don't ignore safety warnings, like announcements or alarms, they are there for a reason.

STAYING SAFE ONLINE

Staying safe online is essential for kids and teenagers. With the rise of technology, the internet has become an integral part of our lives, connecting us to the world and providing us with endless information and resources. However, it's good to be aware of the potential online risks and dangers, such as cyberbullying, hacking, and fraud.

This guide will teach you how to stay safe online, including tips for creating strong passwords, being aware of fake news, and protecting your personal information. By following these safety tips, you can enjoy the benefits of the internet while staying safe and secure.

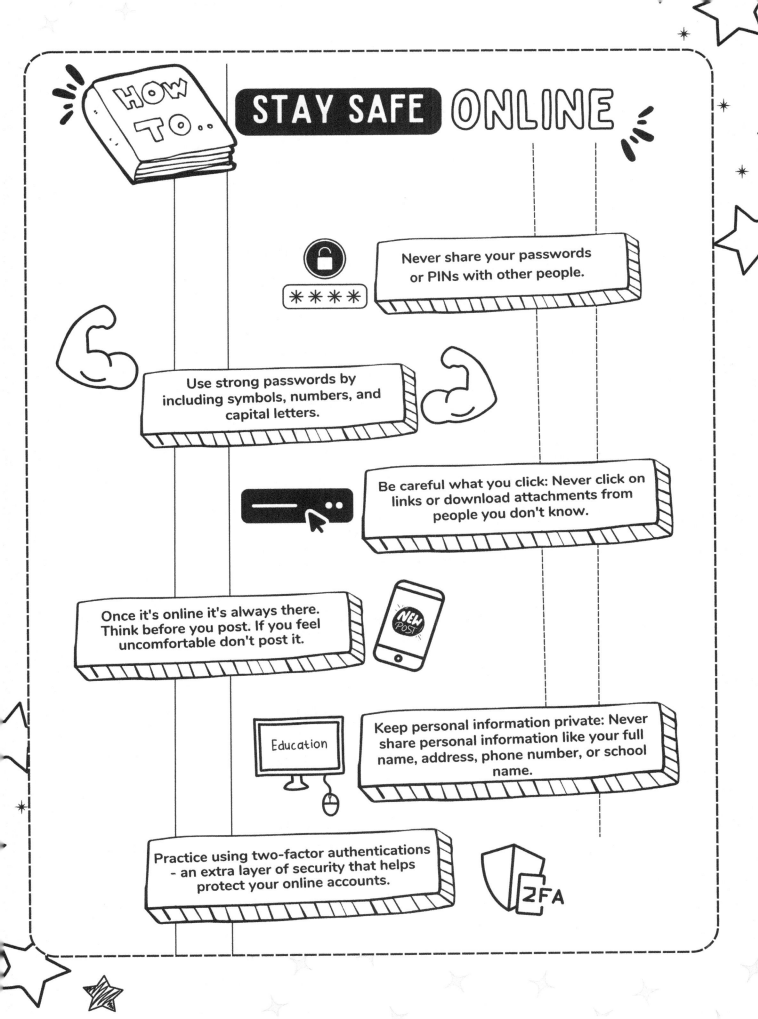

HOW TO... STAY SAFE ONLINE

Never share your passwords or PINs with other people.

Use strong passwords by including symbols, numbers, and capital letters.

Be careful what you click: Never click on links or download attachments from people you don't know.

Once it's online it's always there. Think before you post. If you feel uncomfortable don't post it.

Keep personal information private: Never share personal information like your full name, address, phone number, or school name.

Practice using two-factor authentications - an extra layer of security that helps protect your online accounts.

HOW TO CREATE STRONG PASSWORDS

Passwords are a crucial part of keeping yourself safe online. Almost every site now requires you to use a unique and secure password. So learning how to create strong passwords is essential for keeping your online accounts safe.

But what exactly is a strong password? **A strong password is difficult for others to guess or crack.**

Here are some characteristics of a strong password:

- **Length**: A long password is more complicated to guess than a short one. A password should be 8-12 characters long.

- **Complexity**: A strong password should include a mix of upper and lowercase letters, numbers, and special characters (e.g., !, @, #, $, %).

- **Unpredictability**: Avoid using easily guessable information, such as your name, birthdate, or common words. Instead, use a random combination of characters.

- **Uniqueness**: Each of your accounts should have a unique password. Avoid reusing the same password for multiple accounts.

- **Avoid personal information**: Avoid using personal information that can be easily found, like your name, address, phone number, or family member's name.

- **Avoid common patterns**: Avoid patterns like qwerty, 123456, abcdef, or anything else that can be easily guessed.

An excellent way to create a strong password is to use a passphrase, a string of words, or a sentence that you can easily remember but would be difficult for others to guess.

For example, "I$tormyW3ather@2pm" is a strong password. It is long, has mixed characters, and is not easily guessable.

It's important to remember that a strong password is only effective if you keep it safe and don't share it with anyone. It's also good practice to change your password every few months.

STRONG PASSWORDS

Creating strong passwords helps keep you stay safe online.

WHAT MAKES A STRONG PASSWORD?

1. **Length**: longer the better.
2. **Complexity**: Include upper and lowercase letters, numbers, and special characters (e.g., !, @, #, $, %).
3. **Uniqueness**: Avoid using the same password everywhere.
4. **Avoid personal information**: Avoid using your name, address, phone number, or family members' name.
5. **Avoid common patterns**: Avoid common patterns like qwerty, 123456, abcdef, or anything that can be easily guessed.

ACTIVITY

Circle the strongest passwords below:

YV&yegv3!   jenny   password123

123456   SkuSA2X@$c

feb211998

abc123

AngusEats3Bones!   BigDaddy

HOW TO CREATE STRONG PASSWORDS

Now let's try to create some strong passwords using longer, memorable words.

STEP 1 Write down your favorite animal.

_____

_____

STEP 2 Write down your favorite food.

_____

_____

STEP 3 Write down your age.

_____

_____

STEP 4 Add an uppercase and a symbol

_____

_____

STEP 5 Now combine them all together.

MY PASSWORD IS...

*You can cut out this page and keep this password somewhere safe if you intend to use this later on.

HOW TO SPOT FAKE NEWS

Fake news is a big problem in today's world. It is information that is not true but is presented as real. It can be spread through the internet, social media, and even traditional news sources.

Knowing how to spot fake news is important, so you don't accidentally believe something that isn't true.

Fake news can be hard to spot because it can look similar to real information. Sometimes it's written to be funny or to make people click on it, but it can also trick people into believing something that isn't true. This can be dangerous because it can spread misinformation and cause confusion.

For example, a story that claims that a particular food is harmful when it is not, or a story that says a celebrity is dead when they are not.

There are several ways to detect fake news:

- **Check the source**: Look for familiar and reputable sources, such as well-established news outlets and fact-checking websites. Be skeptical of information from sources you don't recognize or have a history of publishing false information.

- **Verify the information**: Check if other reputable sources report the same information. Use fact-checking websites such as Snopes, FactCheck.org, and PolitiFact to verify the information.

- **Look for evidence**: Check the story for quotes, statistics, and other information that can be verified. If the story lacks evidence, it may be fake.

- **Check the date**: Make sure the story is recent and not a rehashed or outdated story being passed off as new.

- **Check the tone**: Be wary of sensationalist headlines or stories that elicit strong emotions, such as fear or anger. These are often used to spread fake news.

- **Check the context**: Understand the context of the story. Many fake news stories lack context and don't provide a broader understanding of the issue.

Using these methods, you can better evaluate the information you come across and make more informed decisions about what to trust and ignore.

It's important to remember that fake news is not only found in written articles but also in videos, images, and audio recordings. So, it's essential to be critical and verify any content before sharing it.

HOW TO SPOT
FAKE NEWS

With the help of an adult, try to find a news story on social media that seems unbelievable.
Write the news title & source below, then answer the questions with a checkmark or cross.

WHAT IS THE NEWS TITLE & SOURCE?

CHECKLIST		
◉ Check the source: Is the source (website) credible?		
◉ Verify the info: Google the story. Are other sites reporting the info?		
◉ Look for evidence: Can you verify info within the story - stats, quotes etc.?		
◉ Check the date: Is it recent?		
◉ Listen to your gut: What does your gut say? Does it feel real?		

- 3-4 Checkmarks indicate that the info is likely not fake.
- Less than 2 checkmarks indicate that the information may well be fake.

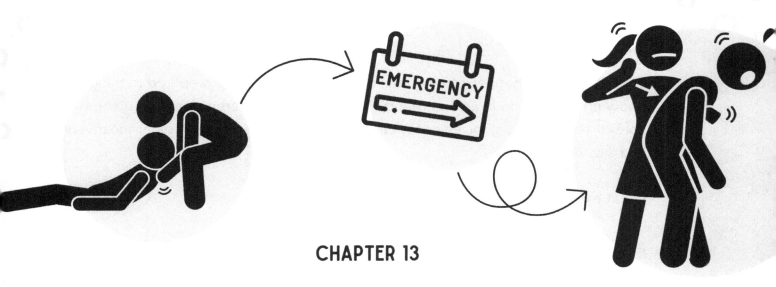

CHAPTER 13

EMERGENCIES
&
FIRST AID

Emergencies can happen at any time, and it's essential to be prepared to handle them. Knowing what to do in an emergency can make a big difference in the outcome. Being able to handle emergencies can mean the difference between a minor inconvenience and a severe injury.

What exactly are emergencies?

An emergency situation is a sudden, unexpected event that requires immediate action to protect yourself or someone else. Emergency situations can be natural disasters, such as a hurricane or flood, or they can be caused by accidents, such as a car crash or a fire. They can also be caused by medical issues, such as a heart attack or a broken bone.

For example, imagine you're playing at the park with friends, and one of them falls and hurts their arm. If you know basic first aid and what to do in an emergency, you'll be able to help your friend until an adult arrives.

HOW TO PREPARE FOR EMERGENCIES

Preparing for emergencies is a crucial step in being able to handle them. This includes learning basic first aid, having emergency contact information, and a plan in case of a natural disaster or other emergency situations.

If an emergency arises, try to stay calm and follow some basic principles:

- **Call the emergency services**. This will alert the proper authorities and get help on the way as soon as possible.

- **Keep the injured person still and comfortable until help arrives**. Cover them with a blanket if they are cold, and do your best to keep them talking and reassuring them.

- **Perform any necessary first aid for injuries**. If you have some basic first-aid experience, use your knowledge to ensure the person is stable.

- **Stay in contact with the emergency services**. They will provide you with all the information and support you need, so stay on the line when possible.

- **Keep yourself safe from danger** by staying away from harmful areas. If the emergency is due to a natural disaster like an earthquake or flood, stay away from falling debris, rising water, and other dangerous areas.

- **Gather as much information as possible** to pass along to the emergency services when they arrive. This includes any medical conditions or allergies of the injured person, details about the location of the accident, and a description of what happened.

By following these basic principles in an emergency situation, you will be able to provide the best possible help and support until trained professionals arrive.

Emergencies can happen anytime, so it's good to be prepared for anything! With practice and knowledge, you'll feel confident and capable of handling any crisis. So let's get started on learning how to be prepared for emergencies.

BE PREPARED!

It's good to be prepared. Above is an empty first aid box. Illustrate, draw or write all the items you might need in an emergency.

FIRST AID

HELPING HAND

How well could you handle an emergency? Look at the injuries on the left and match them to the appropriate treatment.

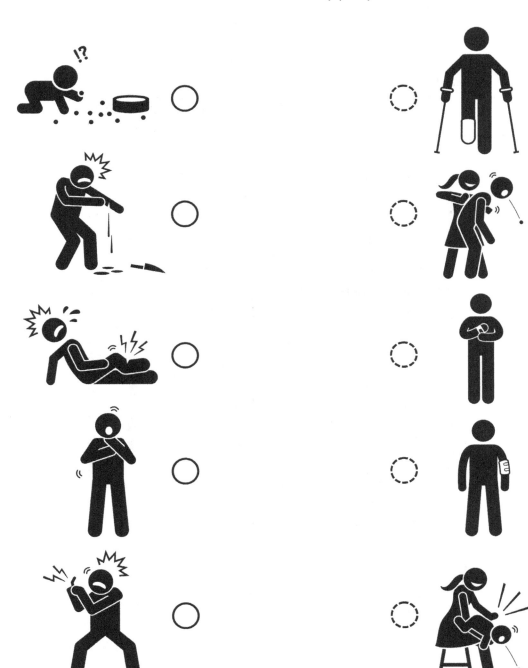

A-MAZE-ING RACE

Help the patient reach the hospital. Navigate the ambulance through the maze.

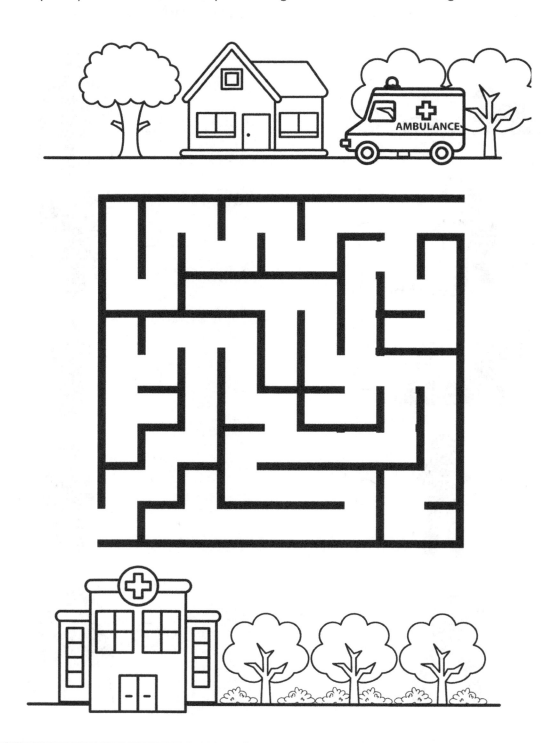

WORD HUNT

Directions: Find all words related to first aid and encircle them. List the words you found below as well. Clue: There are 9 possible words.

D K D U G T M Q A Y D R N J F
L I F A B N A Z G M I W A Q I
O Y U R G E K A K P A Q G D R
Q Z W M U M W F G L D U K U S
E D W S V T P Y C U N B X P T
J R T L P N V O P S A P L D A
C W J I C I H J H E B I R E I
Q G L N B O I K V O N A Z X D
Q E V G L R A H I T Z T A W Y
I H M G Q C H T W I E E O H Z
I A P T R X J S F U A B L B M
T F C E L R O S S I C S Q E C
T Y T J W N L T N J E F G K A
H A J F L L X Z E R S U X Z P
W E N X I L N Y R X I U T T E

ANSWERS:

1. _____

2. _____

3. _____

4. _____

5. _____

6. _____

7. _____

8. _____

9. _____

CHAPTER 14

ADVENTURE SKILLS

> Adventure skills are a great way to get out and explore while building self-confidence and problem-solving abilities.

Building camps and dens and enjoying the wilderness can be incredibly rewarding and fun. It's a way to escape the distractions of technology and reconnect with the natural world. Plus, it's a great way to stay active and healthy.

For example, imagine building a shelter out of branches and leaves or starting a fire using only natural materials.

Not only will you learn valuable skills, but you'll also discover the sense of accomplishment that comes with completing a challenging task.

Adventure skills also allow you to learn about the natural world and understand the importance of conservation. You will learn about the different plants and animals that call the wilderness home and how to respect and protect them.

This chapter will explore different adventure skills, such as building a shelter, starting a fire, and using a map and compass. So, whether you're a beginner or an experienced adventurer, this guide will help you to safely and responsibly explore the great outdoors.

HOW TO USE A MAP & COMPASS

A map and compass are essential tools for any adventurer. They can help you navigate and find your way in the wilderness and allow you to safely explore new areas.

A map represents an area, showing things like roads, trails, bodies of water, and landmarks. Maps come in different scales, offering various levels of detail. *For example, a topographic map shows the terrain and elevations of an area. In contrast, a road map focuses on the roads and major landmarks.*

A compass, on the other hand, is a tool that helps you figure out which direction you're facing. It has a needle that always points to the magnetic north. This allows you to orient your map and determine which direction you need to go to reach your destination.

To use a map and compass together:

- **First, orient your map to match the direction you are facing** by aligning the compass needle with the north arrow on the map.
- **Then, use the compass to determine the direction you need to go** to reach your destination.
- **Use the map to identify landmarks and terrain features along the way.**

By learning to use a map and compass, you'll be able to safely and confidently explore new areas and better understand the natural world around you.

Have a go at completing the adventure worksheets on the following pages. You'll be an explorer in no time. Good luck!

COMPASS POINTS

READING A COMPASS

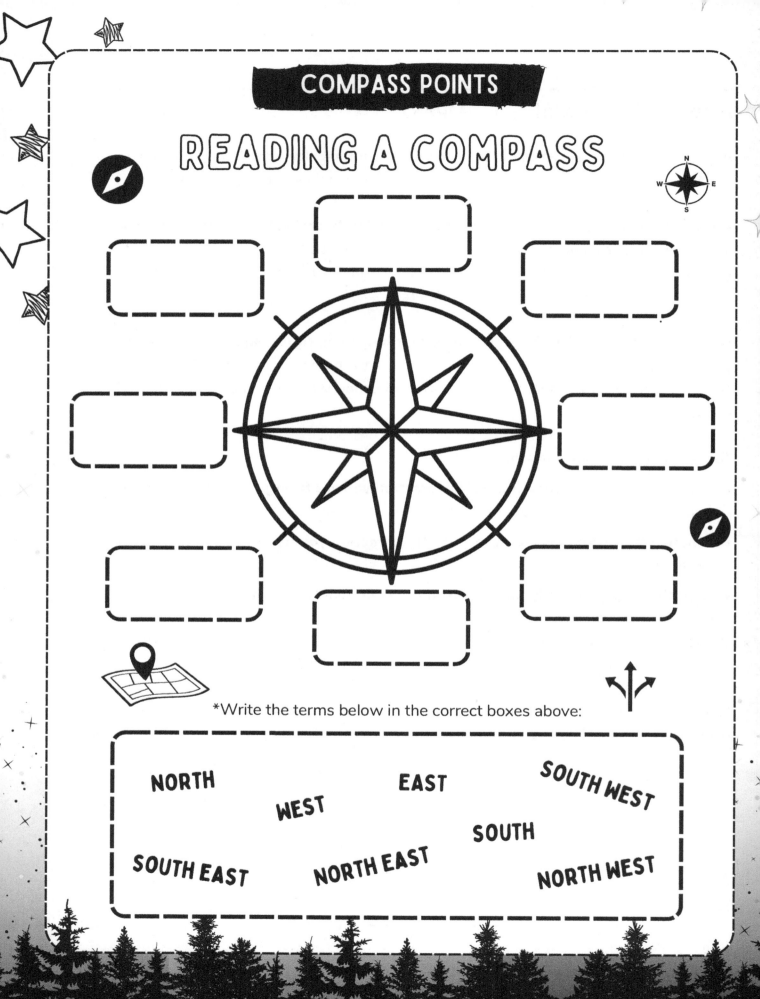

*Write the terms below in the correct boxes above:

NORTH　　　　EAST　　　　SOUTH WEST

WEST

SOUTH

SOUTH EAST　　　NORTH EAST　　　NORTH WEST

USING A MAP, LEGEND & COMPASS

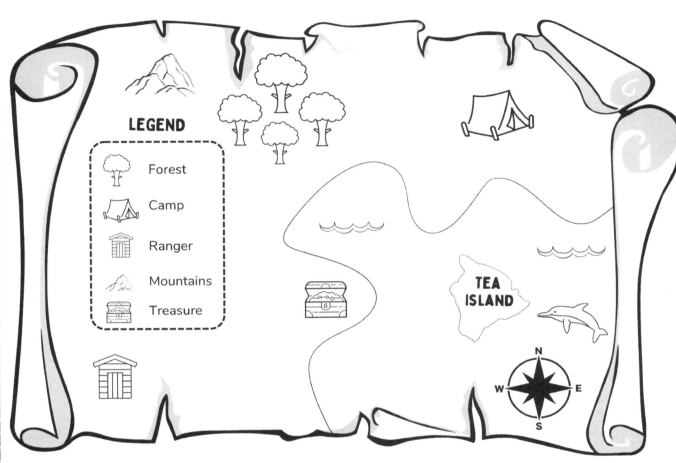

Use directions (north, south, east & west) to answer the questions.

1. The forest is _____ from the camp.

2. The mountains are _____ from the treasure.

3. Tea Island is _____ from the camp.

4. If you were at the camp, what places would you see if you walked west?

5. Color the map to show the water.

BUILD YOUR OWN CAMPFIRE

Put your campfire-building skills to the test! Read through the steps below and number them in the correct order.

Use the twigs, sticks and branches to build a kindling teepee around the tinder.

As your fire grows, add on more dry twigs and branches, and eventually, start feeding it with larger pieces of firewood. Leave some space to allow sufficient airflow.

Choose a safe location. Then make a loose pile of tinder. Don't pack them too tightly. Your fire needs airflow gaps.

To safely put out your fire, you must cut off one of the elements of the Fire Triangle. You can do it by dousing the fire with water or covering it with sand. You can also let the firewood burn out (just be sure there's no fuel surrounding the area to avoid it from catching fire again.)

Being very careful, light the tinder from all sides using your lighter or some matches.

*Fires can be dangerous. You should only ever build a fire under adult supervision.

MASTER CAMPER

You're going for a camping trip with your best friend but you forgot your tent! Draw your perfect outdoor den!

FOOTPRINTS IN THE FOREST

Draw a line between the footprint and the animal that left them.

VACATION ADVENTURES

This is your very own vacation bucket list! Tick-off each activity you do while on vacation.

Build and sleep in a den inside using furniture, sheets & cushions

Find an animal print

Make a treasure map!

Sleep under the stars! Camp out for a night (under adult supervision)

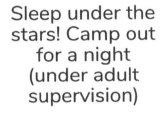

Find the the North Star in the night sky

Build a campfire (with an adult)

Switch off your phone for 24 hours

Watch the sunrise

Find plants in your garden for every colour of the rainbow

LET'S TRAVEL!

YOU'RE ON VACATION

Illustrate the things you might need to take for a summer adventure vacation.

YOU'VE GOT THIS

Congratulations on making it to the end of this workbook on life skills! This book has been designed to support and help you develop the skills required to become successful as a teen and adult.

You've learned about a wide range of topics, from personal safety, budgeting, and cooking to communication, adventure skills, and emergency preparedness. With all the knowledge and tips you've gained; hopefully, you are better prepared to take on any challenge that comes your way and are on your way to becoming a confident and capable individual.

Remember, life is full of surprises and adventures. You'll have good times and bad times, but no matter what comes your way, never give up. Keep growing and learning, and live life to the fullest.

We hope this workbook has been helpful on your journey! Best of luck!

Goodbye, and have fun! :)

LIKED THIS BOOK?
WE THINK YOU'LL
LOVE THESE!

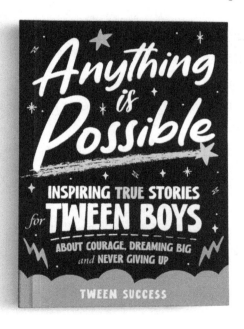

Get your copy

SCAN HERE

BEFORE
YOU GO...

I hope you enjoyed the activities in this book and that you and your child will benefit from implementing the Life Skills discussed.

I would be <u>so</u> grateful if you could leave an honest review or a star rating on Amazon.
(A star rating only takes a couple of clicks!)

Your review helps other parents discover this book and will also be good Karma for you. :)

SCAN HERE
to leave a review

Made in United States
Orlando, FL
08 June 2024

47653501R00096